WHERE DID EVERYBODY GO?

PAUL MOLLOY

Where Did Everybody Go?

1981
DOUBLEDAY & COMPANY, INC.
GARDEN CITY, NEW YORK

"The Twelve Steps" from Alcoholics Anonymous copyright © 1939 by Alcoholics Anonymous World Services, Inc. Reprinted by permission of Alcoholics Anonymous World Services, Inc.

Material from the book HOW DRINKING CAN BE GOOD FOR YOU, by Morris E. Chafetz, copyright © 1976, reprinted with permission of Stein and Day Publishers.

"My Life on the Rocks" by Wilbur Mills, reprinted with permission from The Saturday Evening Post Company © 1979.

The editorial "No to Drunkathons," reprinted courtesy of the Chicago Tribune.

Excerpts from "Alcoholism: New Victims, New Treatment," reprinted by permission from TIME, The Weekly Newsmagazine; Copyright Time Inc. 1974.

Excerpts from THE TIMES OF MY LIFE, by Betty Ford, Copyright © 1978 by Betty Ford. Reprinted by permission of Harper & Row, Publishers, Inc.

Material from I'LL QUIT TOMORROW, by Vernon E. Johnson, D.D. Copyright © 1973 by Vernon E. Johnson, D.D. Reprinted by permission of Harper & Row, Publishers, Inc.

Library of Congress Cataloging in Publication Data

Molloy, Paul.
Where did everybody go?
1. Alcoholism—Biography. 2. Molloy, Paul.
3. Alcoholics Anonymous. I. Title.
RC565.M58   616.86'1'00924 [B]
ISBN: 0-385-04997-8
Library of Congress Catalog Card Number 79-6605

To Dr. Charles L. Anderson
for Saving My Life

WHERE DID EVERYBODY GO?

ONE

I was flat on my back and a woman had fallen on top of me. It was when the balloon popped—I remember this vividly—that I moaned in disgust, "For God's sake, what am I doing here?"

I was playing volleyball in the hospital gymnasium, but it was not a typical game. For one thing, the players consisted of myself and fourteen women, who represented the majority of patients in the hospital's psychiatric ward. There were three other men in that ward, but one had been excused from the game—it was part of physical therapy—because he'd had shock treatment that morning. Another was benched because, as I learned later, he tried to enliven previous games by thumping female bottoms instead of the ball (which didn't strike me as really abnormal behavior). The third escaped the disaster by pleading a sore back.

Adding to the bedlam was the fact that the volleyball normally used for these encounters had exhaled and all but expired, and since there was no pump to inflate it, the male nurse who organized these saturnalia and acted as referee had come up with a green balloon.

Anyone who hasn't engaged in such pandemonium has something missing in his life. Here I was, lone man in this grotesque ballet, with a gaggle of females lofting a sweat-soaked balloon amid the cacophony of the referee's whistle. What, indeed, was I doing here?

Just that week, in the course of my job as a newspaper columnist, I had interviewed Carol Channing, discussed the raising of children with Bobby Kennedy, lunched with Lawrence Welk and cocktailed a bit too long with an ambitious matron who wanted me to guide her career on television (and was to commit suicide a week later). Now I was pursuing a balloon with fourteen females in various stages of neurosis.

It was, at the very least, incongruous.

It was all that, and more, when the balloon soared my way and the big-bosomed, red-haired amazon, uttering a shriek, leaped to intercept it. We collided in midair and dropped to the floor with a thud that fluttered the net. The balloon burst. My teammate disentangled her body from mine, helped me to my feet, and volunteered an unnerving non sequitur that remains etched in my mind: "My husband's a real jerk. Have you met him yet?"

I could think of little to say except that I hadn't had the pleasure. I limped off the court and she followed, her high-pitched words bouncing off the walls of the gymnasium. "Yeah," she went on, "a real creep. He should be here instead of me, know what I mean?"

At that moment I was less than enchanted with her problem and I wished she would go away. But she wouldn't, and for reasons that escape me she apparently decided that we were to be friends and confidants during our stay in the ward.

Mercifully, since we were left with only a shred of rubber, the collision brought an end to volleyball, or volleyballoon, for that day. I had no particular distaste for the game—though playing with a platoon of emotionally disturbed women did cramp my style—but I deplored the regimentation of patients during these various excursions.

When it was time for a walk, everyone had to walk. When it was time to bowl, everyone had to go bowling. When it was time for a movie in the ward, everyone had to sit through the movie. (I don't care if I never see an airlines travelog again.) When it was time for a popcorn party, a sing along, or an art class, everyone had to pop corn (or at least eat some), warble "Moonlight Bay," or do a still-life sketch of pomegranates (though not, thank God, at the same time). When it was time to swim, even if one carried the world's woes on one's shoulders, the overpowering suggestion was "Everybody in the pool."

On the surface these appear to be minor concerns, and indeed they are, but in a locked psychiatric ward they assume vast significance because almost everything the patient says or does is carefully heeded and entered on his chart, where, next morning, it is scrutinized, analyzed and categorized by an assemblage of psychiatrists, psychologists, counselors, nurses and their aides, visiting doctors, students on field trips and other assorted observers.

During one of our popcorn poppings, for example, there developed a disagreement which very nearly led to a hairpulling bacchanal that had me trying to soothe an excess of ladies in the kitchen. I envisioned the entry on my chart:

> Ointment applied to Paul M.'s elbow for burn sustained in argument in kitchen during popcorn party. Argument started when Mary F. protested that Estelle S. used too much butter on kernels, creating a calorie problem. Tempers flared when Shirley B. insisted that salting should occur during popping, not after. Eugenia R. then accused Alice McV. of making off with the larger popcorn balls for a necklace she is making for her niece. Meanwhile, Robert N. pushed Joan C. when Joan tried to pour dye into pan to color popcorn pink (day shift

should check how Joan got hold of dye). In scuffle, Paul was
shoved against hot plate and burned elbow.

During other hospitalizations—there were many—I became embroiled frequently in what could be described as
The Battle of Occupational Therapy.

While I recognize the need for occupational therapy
(O.T.), I detest it in every form. I am not adept with my
hands, to the point where straightening a picture on the
wall is an achievement. With absolutely no pride, I admit
that seldom have I changed the ribbon in a typewriter during the thirty-five years I have used it to make a living. As a
handyman I have all the grace of a pregnant giraffe in
quicksand.

Since I saw little future in the individual production of
such items as ashtrays, I made it a point to use all the cunning at my command to avoid going to the O.T. room,
which I found a veritable Chamber of Horrors.

For the most part, I was able to convince psychiatrists
that reading was the best O.T. for me. I am an avid reader
and, when out of standard reading matter, have managed
to regale myself by studying the labels on mayonnaise jars.
Caught without a paper on the bus, I have found bliss in a
billboard for cough drops. My idea of luscious O.T. in the
hospital is a towering pile of books and magazines and,
should I reach the bottom of the pile, I think I could enjoy
the instructions on the urine-specimen kit and fantasize
over the unheralded author.

But in these endeavors I had a notable lack of success
with the nurses, especially male nurses, who were generally
in charge of activities outside the ward. Time and again I
would tell them the doctor had given me permission to stay
in my room and read, but there usually was a skirmish.
Somehow the doctor's recommendation in my case—I always made myself a special case—had not filtered down to

the male nurses (whom I annoyed by calling turnkeys or keepers). So they would galumph into my room with their little lists and proclaim, with entirely too much zeal:

"Well, are we ready for O.T. today?"

"No."

Then, with the hint of a smirk, they would add:

"And today's the day we finish our ashtrays, isn't it?"

"No."

They knew I hated making ashtrays, and birdhouses, and leather belts and moccasins.

So there would follow a battle of wits during which I would dredge up any lie or excuse that might save me from having to leave the ward. If my clout with the doctor seemed of no avail, I would feign various pains and symptoms. I once used a blue crayon on my thumb to fake a sprain; that didn't work, so the next day I simulated tears to prove I was in a depression and too despondent to lace tatters of buckskin into moccasins. But the turnkeys knew all the tricks.

In time I learned that the best way for a patient to avoid the Chamber of Horrors was to stay out of his room, where the keeper could break down his resistance in privacy, and take refuge in the ward's smoking room. I called this room Emphysema Annex, and its main attraction was an electric wall lighter whose receptacle looked a little like the mouthpiece on old-fashioned telephones. To unnerve a new nurse on the ward, especially one looking for odd behavior, I sometimes found it amusing to stand in front of the mouthpiece and rasp, "Operator! About that call to Pittsburgh—can I get through now?"

Since patients in psychiatric wards are not allowed to carry matches or lighters, and since smoking was not permitted elsewhere, Emphysema Annex was a popular rendezvous. There was some safety in numbers, because our keepers did not like to confront a stubborn patient in front of his peers. A hassle between the nurse and a patient who did not want to go for a group walk could create discordant vibes among the tightly knit group in Emphysema Annex and jar the whole ward into a brabble. The doctors on their rounds could sense such dissension immediately.

Thus, a patient who felt out of sorts could seclude himself within the fog of cigarette smoke and say, "No, I don't feel like building a bookshelf this morning because I threw up after breakfast and I heard from my brother who has cancer and I'm shook up because they won't give me a weekend pass and I want to stay here because I'm expecting an important phone call from my wife (husband, son, daughter, father, mother, landlord, lawyer, creditors and so on)."

The nurses could demolish shallow subterfuge like that if they were alone with the sophist, but to try it where fellow sufferers would rally to the patient's support would mark them as barbarians with quartz for hearts.

Another neat ruse was to have the hocus initiated by a roommate, with the scenario usually being the same. Say that Miriam didn't feel like exercising on the silly bicycle that went nowhere, and wanted to put up her hair or watch a soap opera on television. She would skip breakfast, at about which time her roommate would sigh, within earshot of a hovering nurse:

"I'm worried about Miriam; she's not herself today."

Someone else at the table would join in:

"Yeah, she's acting kind of strange."

Others would then make contributions like, "She's been peculiar since she got that phone call yesterday," or "I tried to talk her out of it but she won't react."

In very little time these sympathetic cluck-clucks would find their way to the nurses' station, setting the stage for whatever artful humbug Miriam had dreamed up, and she was home free.

Often the chief of staff, or whoever was in charge of the ward, could gather valuable information on the progress or regress of patients from the interplay of emotions and moods stemming from the near similarity of their problems, their response, or their insensibility to one another's welfare.

An example was induced by an oaf in the ward whose behavior had become unbearable. He was almost the stereotype of the old breed of hippies—swaggering, unkempt, with uncombed hair, pubescent beard and an obvious aversion to soap. He spent hours with his ear against the stereo tuned to those radio stations that dispense only high-decibel rock. A bit of a bully, he had a drug problem, and the only civility he showed was toward a soiled guitar that lacked one string and any rapport with the owner.

In the room adjoining his was a gentle old lady, a tranquil antique we called Sneaky Sal. She suffered from, among other things, narcolepsy and was forever sneaking off to her bed to sleep. Occasionally, when the nurses locked her out of her room, she would slink to some other inmate's room and curl up under the covers.

It reached a point where she was propped up in a chair with a bedsheet corseted around her waist so she would not scamper off to play musical beds. Despite the makeshift jerkin, she had no trouble dropping off into placid slumber.

When I found her faintly sobbing one morning, she whispered that she could no longer stand the endless rataplan from the stereo. Many times she had asked the barefoot vulgarian to turn it down, but he had ignored her. In fact, she said, he had become insolent and she was terrified of him.

I, too, could no longer take the caterwaul. During breakfast I walked over to the stereo and turned it off, telling the young clod that if he turned it on again to those stations I would break his back. That was all.

Less than an hour later, as we awaited the doctor's rounds, I heard a commotion in the dayroom. It was the chief psychiatrist on his hands and knees, literally wrenching the mechanism out of the stereo. Part of the entrails were on the floor, and he growled to the head nurse standing beside him, "I've told you about this before, but you've done nothing about it!"

What makes the incident meaningful is that none of the principals involved in the pother—not I, nor Sneaky Sal, nor the unwashed dolt, nor any other patient—had told the doctor about it. Yet our tense feelings, or Sneaky Sal's agitation, had somehow filtered back to him. There was simply an awareness on his part that all was not well in the ward, and he did something about it.

The rumpus spawned two fringe benefits. Sneaky Sal regained her composure, though perhaps too well. She became so relaxed that she returned to her zombielike state and in time became the only person I've ever known who could masticate liver and onions while asleep.

Further, the exorcism of the stereo brought about a change in the owner of the crippled guitar. He established a decent relationship with Sneaky Sal and eventually rallied to my side during my ordeals in the Chamber of Horrors.

Those interludes in O.T., though important and necessary, were a veritable purgatory for me.

First I was assigned—against my will, of course—to making moccasins. In vain I threw every objection I could think of at my turnkey:

"I'm allergic to buckskin. My great-grandfather was part Indian." (That happened to be true, but it made no dent.)

"There's no future in this kind of footwear anyway. Even Eskimo don't wear these things."

"My eyesight's not good. I'm lousy on precision work."

Nothing worked—except me. I worked on moccasins.

But I determined I wouldn't be on moccasins for long. I set to work with a vengeance (we looked like those little elves in Santa's workshop) until I began hearing whispers of how well I was becoming adjusted. Snip, clip, thread. Snip, clip, thread. After each session I'd stash my supply of moccasins away in an abandoned locker and soon I was winning glances of approval from staff members.

At the end of the week, I took my supply out of the locker and dropped it on the O.T. director's workbench. His approval quickly turned to dismay. "There's something wrong with this stuff," he said. "Good grief, they're all for the left foot!"

They were indeed. I had devised a way to shape the contour in the same arc on every last one of them. "I told you I have lousy eyesight," I said.

"That's all for you on moccasins," he rumbled.

Good, I thought. Now I can go back to my reading.

"Starting Monday," the director boomed, "you go on birdhouses."

I took pains on that job. Hammers and saws and nails and all those tools are foreign to me, but I became the dedicated architect. The sides of the birdhouse were even, the base was sturdy and the roof slanted at just the right angle. I even volunteered a special touch and painted it gray. Only one thing was missing from my masterpiece: It had no hole.

The director sneered, "And how will the birds get in and out?"

"It's for woodpeckers," I said. "They'll know what to do."

The story of my doorless birdhouse for woodpeckers went the rounds of the ward, and at dinnertime the stout lady with whom I'd collided during the volleyball game said admiringly, "You sure outfoxed them. You don't belong in this squirrel cage."

That night, unable to sleep, I found myself agreeing with her. I had checked into the hospital for "exhaustion," a convenient diagnosis for ten days of serious drinking, but the hospital did not have an alcoholism-rehabilitation unit at the time. My doctor asked me if I'd mind going into the psychiatric ward, where detoxification facilities were available. I had agreed, but was now having second (and soberer) thoughts.

This was a place for neurotics, psychotics and depressives. The redhead was right. I didn't belong with emotionally sick people. I might have a drinking problem, but I wasn't sick. Certainly I would transfer to the medical ward first thing in the morning.

I had no way of knowing that night that my decision to stay where I was would trigger the small miracle that eventually would save my life.

TWO

Four new patients, three men and a woman, checked in (staggered in, really) the next day, and it was obvious they had arrived with a drinking problem. I soon learned that five of the other seventeen patients had also had run-ins with Old Popskull, which meant there were nine alcoholics or potential alcoholics in the ward. To have included myself would have given the membership a neat round total of ten; but I had no intention of becoming part of the fermented clan, though I had decided to stay a few days to dry out.

Still, something—perhaps it was the muzzy effects of the Valium that was sedating us—drew us together and we found ourselves exchanging stories about elbow-bending. I found one session so entertaining that I would occasionally dart to my room to make hurried notes. I didn't know why I was making notes; perhaps it was professional instinct.

While training for an upcoming prizefight, former champion Joe Louis was once asked about his opponent's defensive skills; the contender was famous for "bicycling" —backing up to tire his rival. Louis uttered (or borrowed) what has become a classic comment: "He can run, but he can't hide."

If that boxer had been an alcoholic, he probably could have dethroned the champion because alcoholics, I learned during the gabfests, have an uncanny talent for hiding their problem. The energy they exert to conceal the booze from a suspicious world is immeasurable, and the planning they engage in to keep their sustenance out of sight sometimes borders on genius.

The beginning alcoholic soon learns to shun the obvious hiding places. No tosspot in his right mind (ignore the contradiction) will long tuck a jug of the gargle under his shirts in the dresser, behind the bookshelf or amid old magazines in the basement. Even an unsuspecting wife would get to those nooks sooner or later during her chores.

But the drinking wife has an advantage at home; unless the nipping has turned to guzzling, and her husband is on the scent, she can get by for a time with a mundane cache like the nest where she lays her underthings. Unless they have some aberration, most men will not go riffling into brassieres and panty hose.

So eventually the "blue ruin" finds its way from clothes hampers into the assorted bottles that a woman comes into contact with each day, from tiny perfume flasks for short nips to cologne bottles in the bathroom, to cruets in the kitchen that normally hold vinegar and serve as the perfect receptacle for vodka.

It should be noted that just about every female alcoholic will discover early in the game the delightful secrecy of the toilet tank. For reasons I can't explain, this cool bower is preferred by women more than by men, though one patient told me he once used it, only to make a startling discovery.

"My wife found my hiding place," he said. "I used to put the stuff inside the spare in the car trunk, but she found it. So one night I decided to use the commode.

"I always figured toilet tanks were for amateurs, but I was in a rush and I couldn't think of a better place, so I lifted the lid on the tank and was about to drop in my bottle, and what do you think I found in there? Another bottle.

"That's how I found out my wife had started drinking on the sly. We talked about it and she told me she used to hide her supply at the bottom of the diaper pail. Then the kid grew out of diapers and she went for the toilet. Strictly amateur. But that was years ago and she's been dry a long time now."

I heard a stranger charade involving a man and wife who overindulged, but in this case the wife did not have a drinking problem. She, an enormity, belonged to Overeaters Anonymous, and he, an architect, was an alcoholic with a snuggery that should have been foolproof. His ruse was to stow his liquor inside the spacious pocket of an old army coat stashed at the rear of the clothes closet. Since the garment was a memento of his wartime exploits, he was sure his wife would hold it sacred and untouchable, a sort of rumpled shrine to his patriotism.

And so it hung until one morning, when he went to the coat for reinforcements. But the hangover tilted his coordination, and when he thrust a shaky hand into the pocket he came up with a fistful of chocolate bars.

He had put his hand into the wrong pocket, the one his wife had been using to hide the candy she wasn't supposed to touch. Both were playing the same game of duplicity, and now, because of a retired overcoat, they were tied.

As the stories unfolded, I thought the prize for ingenuity might go to one fellow who managed to outwit his wife for months with a deceptively simple maneuver—a buried bottle and a straw. Next to drinking, his favorite hobby was tending his lawn and shrubbery on weekends, and every Saturday and Sunday he managed to indulge both hobbies to the fullest.

Each Saturday at noon, as his suspicious wife watched from the veranda, he would trot to the lawn, sober as he'd been all week, and steer his lawnmower up and down the spacious lawn; lie down for a bit of rest and sun; clip the hedges; cut more grass; lie down for more rest and sun; prune the bushes; mow some more; rest some more and so on until sunset, when he would sway back to the house, totter to his bedroom and promptly pass out.

His wife was aquiver with frustration. She knew he had no liquor in the house because over the years she had become familiar with every hiding place. And his grog couldn't be in the bushes because on Saturday nights, when her husband was sleeping it off, she would take a flashlight and poke through the landscape, coming up with nothing but a monumental huff. Yet the next day, Sunday, as soon as the couple would return from church, the hungover sot would change into his slacks and become the gentleman farmer again. Some Sunday nights he wouldn't even make it to the porch.

One Saturday, however, as he was going about his chores, he lay down for his usual rest and sun for about the sixth time that afternoon and got too much of both. His wife found him totally swacked, with a plastic straw in his mouth, the other end of the straw leading to the bottom of a bottle of bourbon. Sobered up the next day and aware that the game was up, he explained his stratagem: Every Friday afternoon, while she was getting her hair done, he would plant bottles in strategic holes in the lawn deep enough so that the neatly clipped turf canopied the straws. Then on weekends, when it was time to pause in the shearing of the green to take his rest and sun, he would lie on the grass, lay his head over the bottle and, while the sun tanned his back, zestfully suck up the nectar which, the Bible claims, "maketh glad the heart of man."

Another intrepid boozer who also enjoyed outdoing his wife had a certain finesse, but I have grave doubts about his taste—and his liver. He was unemployed, and whenever he was inspired to feign amends, he would put on a morning-after show that deserved marks for originality and guts. Before his wife left for work, he would uncork his bottles and dramatically pour the sauce down the kitchen sink with a flourish. "Look, honey, I'm through with the stuff. Down the drain it goes."

The moment her car was out the driveway he would get a wrench, dismantle the gooseneck beneath the sink and retrieve the liquids that remained in the pipes, rust and all. I had to wonder which was the more corroded, the kitchen ducts or his own.

This trick reminded another patient, a paunchy mailman, of how he'd put up his supply for what must have been the whole winter season. Each fall he stored away two garden hoses in the basement, and on a day when his wife would be gone for some time—the poor fellow did need the time—he would patiently fill both hoses with gin. Whenever the need for a blast came on him, he'd amble downstairs, where, blessedly, he had a workshop, and syphon by mouth whatever swig he needed at the moment. Needless to say, he had bulging eyes, pursed lips and an assortment of colored veins on his cheeks that reminded me of a road map.

"You really had to have your gin, didn't you?" I said.

"Oh, yeah," he said, almost with pride, "and in the daytime, too. You see, mailmen have relay boxes every few miles on the rounds, where we pick up new stacks of mail. I keep a pint in every one of them, so I'm never without a drink."

"And you never got caught, or made the wrong deliveries or anything like that?"

"Never. I'm half-bombed most of the time, but I'm very, very careful on the job."

Neither snow nor rain nor heat nor gloom of night nor booze . . .

A female patient, head of a travel agency, thought we should know about her brother-in-law: "The weirdest I ever heard was what he did. He and my sister had this old stove in the basement, some kind of antique; hadn't been used for years. Well, one day he came home and found my sister had sold it to a junkman for something like five dollars. He was furious; he almost hit her. She told him it was junk and using up space and what the hell was he so mad about.

"Boy, was he mad. He'd been hiding a bottle in that old stove all this time and there was a bottle in there when she sold it. He asked her then and there who the junkman was and where he lived. And do you know what that brother-in-law of mine did? He jumped in his car and drove up to that junk place and bought the stove right back!

"Imagine! He wanted that damned bottle so bad he bought the stove back. For ten dollars! He could have bought a bunch of bottles with that ten dollars. But no, he was so worked up about that missing bottle he paid the guy all that money to get the stove back. He didn't mind his wife knowing about his hiding place, but I guess he was ashamed about the junkman knowing it. Now that's got to be crazy thinking."

No one disagreed, though I was inclined to match that kind of alcoholic behavior with that of the bank executive who always kept an extra pair of shorts in his safe-deposit box because he unfailingly developed a case of the runs at precisely ten o'clock every morning, and he had had too many accidents to ever again report for work (he was a vice-president) without that precaution.

So the stories went—about the fireman who used to hide his bottle inside his high-top boots at the firehouse (I wouldn't want him at my fire).

And the woman who managed to affix her half pints within the foot-high beehive wigs that were the style years ago.

And the accountant who came up with the clever idea of shooting vodka into oranges with a syringe and always kept an orange on his desk. (But why not shoot it into watermelons and tie on a real bun?)

And the truck driver who sheepishly admitted he'd sometimes used his wife's douche bag to hide his liquor. At least he had the candor to add, "I guess that was a little gross . . ."

I wistfully hoped I might share in the hide-the-hootch dialog, but since I didn't see myself as an alcoholic, I kept quiet that night. Later, however, I did contribute a drinking incident that made them nod knowingly.

It had happened to one of my daughters (I have six daughters and two sons) and her girl friend when they were teenagers. My daughter was to drive her friend, Sally, to a medical clinic, where Sally was to deliver a urine specimen because of some ailment she was having diagnosed.

For some reason Sally did not have, nor could she find, a proper container for the specimen. Since the time for the appointment was approaching, she decided to use an empty half-pint bottle her parents had discarded the night before.

She did what she had to do—and it must have taken some doing—and off the girls went to the clinic. But they stopped at a supermarket on the way, and when they returned to the car they discovered that the bottle, which Sally had left on the front seat, was gone. Some miscreant had spotted it through the open window, took it for what it looked like, and made off with it. The image of that poor wretch, probably dying for a pick-me-up, taking a quick swig from the stolen bottle remains with me, and I've wondered if the experience drove him to drink or to sobriety.

A few days later I was talking with an alcoholism counselor—a recovered alcoholic—who was visiting the hospital. I mentioned the horror stories I had heard.

"Those aren't horror stories," he said. "Alcoholics are not 'bad' people. They're sick people. They have a terminal illness, and incurably sick people sometimes think strange and act strange. That business about the vodka in the orange? I was doing that before I hit skid row."

"You were on skid row?"

"Yes. After nearly twenty years of being drunk, and I mean drunk every day. You want to know the shape I was in at the end? I'd have such bad shakes in the morning that I couldn't get a shot or a beer down. Hell, I couldn't even keep a drink of water down. So I gave myself whisky enemas."

"Enemas?"

"Right."

I said I didn't believe him.

"It's true," he said. "I had to get booze in my system or I'd die. But I couldn't keep it down, and I had to get it inside me, in my bloodstream, in a hurry. So I did it with enemas. It worked. Nothing else did."

"And now you're helping other alcoholics?"

He smiled. "I'm helping myself. Doing what I'm doing is what's keeping me sober, one day at a time. For thirteen years."

THREE

I ran into the counselor again a few months later, when I was in another hospital, recovering from what I kept telling myself, and everyone else, was "exhaustion." When he stopped by, I couldn't resist making a wisecrack that had been on my mind since he'd told me about his Bourbon enemas:

"When you were pouring a drink up your rear end, what was the toast? Up the hatch? Bottoms up?"

He laughed, but I had joshed myself into a trap because he returned a few times to talk some more about his drinking escapades and the drinking habit in general. I didn't realize it then, but I know now that while he was relating his drinking problems, he was slyly making me think of mine. Anyone, especially a newsman, would find interesting a man who had recovered from an addiction that had brought him to the brink of death. So I listened when he told me about his favorite "club," Alcoholics Anonymous, though my interest in AA continued to be sluggish and almost indifferent, and I was intrigued by what he told me about a man named William Griffith Wilson. Biography is a favorite game with me, so I took notes, thinking that someday I might write a column about these ex-bums. AA was not for me, however; it was for drunken lowlifes, the misfits with no willpower who wind up in funny farms. But it might be worth a column sometime.

This fellow Wilson plainly fit the picture of the typical swillpot that December morning when he awoke, his mind trying to emerge from a long drunken stupor. The wind outside whistled against the barred windows near his bed. But Wilson didn't hear the wind; instead, as he later told it, he heard what sounded like organ music coming out of the walls. But there was no such music.

How long had he been here? Was it last night that he had taken that last drink? A couple of days perhaps?

Actually, he had been in bed two weeks, alive yet dead to the world he had come to fear and hate. He was in the psychiatric ward of a New York City hospital, dreadfully sick, on the verge of delirium tremens again, and he wanted to die.

And why not? He had wanted to die before, such as the times he had gazed out the windows of tall buildings and studied bottles in his medicine cabinet. Too far gone in drink to want to live and too scared of an appointment with death, he had, by his own admission, been drunk night and day for five years.

He had tried everything—almost everything—to bring an end to his misery. Death was the only way out, but why didn't the damnable thing come and bring an end to it all?

It had begun so simply: A drink to ease the loneliness of nights during the Big War when the doughboys sat in British pubs and sang about the day when Johnny would come marching home. Once home, he became caught up in the maelstrom of Wall Street, where his peculiar talents made him the hero he hadn't been "over there." His drinking by then had become a pleasant habit, but it was continuous. He did not know he was a sick man.

For the next few years fortune threw success and acclaim his way, but drink was now an important part of his life. He had arrived in the business world, but with him had arrived a disease, alcoholism, that subtly began to take its toll. Abruptly, in October 1929, the stockmarket collapsed, the Great Depression was born and Bill Wilson was out of work. But Wall Street had labeled him a brilliant analyst, hadn't it? There would be other jobs. There were, but alcohol had ceased to be a luxury; it was now a necessity.

He was fired from job after job (reluctantly, because he was gifted), then found himself on a downward spiral with nothing to clutch on the way to the bottom. His wife took work in a department store and would come home to find him drunk. Mornings, he had to down a tumbler of gin and four bottles of beer before he could even look at breakfast.

He lost his mortgaged home and sometimes stole cash from his wife's purse when the morning terror and madness were on him. He had to stop, but he couldn't. He went to doctors (his brother-in-law was a sympathetic physician) and clergymen, and was in and out of rest homes, coming out each time with the resolve that this would be the last time.

But it wasn't. He would later recall, "I knew that soon my wife would have to give me over to the undertaker or the asylum. I was drinking two bottles of gin a day, and then three became routine. Where was my high resolve? Was I crazy? No words can tell of the despair and loneliness I found in that morass of self-pity. Quicksand stretched around me in all directions. I had met my match. Alcohol was my master."

At one point in his descent into hell Wilson told his wife not to worry because men of genius conceived their best projects when drunk. He did not know then what a prophecy this was; that one day hundreds of thousands of suffering men and women would speak his name with reverence.

The days in the hospital passed slowly and medication gradually brought clarity to his mind. He began to think of God, but the very word always had aroused antipathy. He could take such conceptions as "creative intelligence," "universal mind," or "spirit of nature," but he resisted the thought of a czar of the heavens.

Now, as he lay in bed, he began to think of what he later described as a novel idea born of a "spiritual experience": Why not choose your own conception of God? Admit you're licked. Get honest with yourself and pray to whatever God you think there is. And he found himself crying out, "If there is a God, let Him show Himself! I'm ready to do anything!" "Suddenly," he later wrote to a friend, "I was caught up in an ecstasy which there are no words to describe. And then it burst upon me that I was a free man. It was only a matter of being willing to believe in a power greater than myself. Nothing more was required of me to make my beginning. In those days in the hospital I admitted for the first time that of myself I was nothing. I was to test my thinking by the new God-consciousness within. Never was I to pray for myself, except as my request bore on my usefulness to others. Only then might I expect to receive."

At this point Wilson became alarmed and called his doctor, asking if perhaps he were having a hallucination. The doctor listened, finally shook his head and said, "Something has happened to you that I don't understand. But you had better hang on to it. Anything is better than the way you were."

While he made his slow recovery, the thought came to Wilson that there were thousands of alcoholics who might be relieved to have what he had been given, and perhaps he could help them. Then they, in turn, might help others.

Released from the hospital, he began talking to other drunks, passing along the philosophy that alcoholism is a disease, an incurable disease, but one that could be arrested; a physical allergy complicated by a mental obsession or turmoil. He discovered that by discussing the problem with others like himself, by thinking about their problem and reaching out to help them, he was changing his own personality and staying away from liquor. Something was working where before nothing had.

Some months later on a trip to Akron, Ohio, he ran into a business setback and almost naturally headed for the hotel bar to forget his disappointment. But then he stopped short, remembered the importance of talking to another drunk, called the first church listed in the lobby directory and asked the pastor to quickly put him in touch with "another boozer." The pastor referred him to a "Dr. Bob," who had been trying for years to end his own compulsive drinking.

"Dr. Bob" agreed, without much enthusiasm, to talk with the stranger "for a few minutes." They talked for six hours, returning again and again to three fundamental thoughts: that alcoholism is a disease in which the body cannot tolerate alcohol, even in small quantities, much as the diabetic cannot take sugar; that the alcoholic must accept the fact that he is a sick person who should, in his own way and without prodding from anyone, turn to a "greater power" than himself; and that the only person an alcoholic will listen to and eventually believe is another alcoholic who has walked the same lonely road.

That was June 10, 1935, and from that meeting Alcoholics Anonymous was born.

In January 1971 the gaunt, twangy-voiced Wilson from

Bedford Hills, New York, died of pneumonia at the age of seventy-five, mourned by a million persons. The mourners are the men and women who are active members of Alcoholics Anonymous, a fellowship of individuals—many of them former human wrecks—who share their experience, strength and hope with each other so that they may solve their common problem and help others recover. Wilson's cofounder of AA, "Dr. Bob," was an Akron surgeon, Dr. Robert Holbrook Smith, who died of cancer in 1950.

After leaving the hospital I went to two AA meetings, but only out of curiosity. That bit about a "spiritual experience" didn't really turn me on. But I was affected enough to ask a few AAs how they achieved sobriety, how they could resist ducking into a bar or taking a drink at a party. Often the answer went something like this: "I'm not sure. All I know is that for me, at least, it works."

Exact figures are impossible, but from what I've heard here and there and read, about 50 percent of those who join AA achieve immediate, permanent sobriety. Another 25 percent suffer relapses ("slips"), falling off the wagon once or many times, but they eventually come back to the fold and remain there. The other 25 percent just don't make it, either because they can't face the prospect of life without alcohol or they are physically too far gone ("wet brain") to let go of the bottle.

One of the AAs I spoke to, a Chicago bone specialist, told me, "I was sure, as a doctor, I could work out the combination of drugs and medicines that would allow me to drink the way I wanted to and still function. For years I tried all the medical tricks, along with the right pills, the insulin, the oxygen tank, the vitamin B_{12} shots—you name it—but they didn't work. After hitting bottom fifteen years ago, I joined AA because I knew that alone I couldn't change the person I was that made me drink. I haven't had a drink since."

I wondered what made one person an alcoholic and another merely a social drinker who could handle liquor. After all, the moderate drinker has little trouble giving up liquor if he feels like it. The hard drinker, too, can stop or moderate if he wants to for, say, health reasons.

From bits and pieces I picked up, I got the impression that the hard drinker is not necessarily an alcoholic, and that many an alcoholic never has been a hard drinker. Or, as one veteran AA put it, "It's not what you drink or how much or how often. It's the dependency and what the stuff does to your personality."

The real alcoholic may start off as a moderate drinker and may or may not become a continuous hard drinker. But at some stage in his drinking career he begins to lose control of his consumption. He may be one of the finest people in the world, but he has an absolute genius for getting tight at exactly the wrong moment, often when some important decision must be made or an engagement kept. He is often perfectly sensible and well balanced concerning everything except liquor, but in that respect he is usually dishonest and selfish.

He often has special abilities and builds up a bright outlook for himself and his family, but then he pulls the structure down with a senseless series of sprees. Why does he behave this way, knowing that one drink means new suffering and humiliation?

The opinions I collected were varied. What is known is that while the alcoholic keeps away from the drench, as he may for months or years, he reacts much like anyone else. But once he takes any alcohol, something happens in the bodily and mental sense that makes it virtually impossible for him to stop. Most medical experts agree that in some persons something organic is awry, although the alcoholic's main problem centers more in his mind than in his body.

He may offer a hundred alibis, many of them plausible, for having taken that first drink, but deep down he really does not know why he did it. One Chicago alcoholic told me he drank only when things went well and life was smiling at him, but never when he was depressed or disappointed. Another said, "I'm a White Sox fan. When they won I'd get stinko for joy, and when they lost that got me stoned, too."

At a certain point in his drinking, I was told, every alcoholic passes into a state where the most powerful desire to stop drinking is of no avail. The fact is that most alcoholics, for reasons still obscure, have lost the power of choice in drink and must succumb to the unexplainable wants of their innards and the strange manipulations of their minds. They are unable at certain times to bring into their consciousness with sufficient force the memory of the misery of even a week or a month ago. They are without defense against that first drink. They have, for the most part, tried every imaginable remedy. There have been brief recoveries, always followed by a still worse relapse. Doctors familiar with the problem agree there is no such thing as making a "normal" drinker out of an alcoholic. Science may one day accomplish this, but it hasn't done so yet.

Here are some of the "cures" alcoholics have tried: drinking only beer or wine; limiting the number of drinks; never drinking alone; never drinking in the forenoon; drinking only at home; never having it in the house; never drinking during working hours; drinking only at parties or on weekends; switching from scotch to brandy or from Bourbon to wine; agreeing to resign if ever found drunk on the job; taking a trip; not taking a trip; swearing off drink forever (with or without a solemn oath); doing more physical exercise; reading inspirational books; returning to church; going to health farms and sanitariums; accepting voluntary commitment to asylums, and on and on.

At one of the two AA meetings I attended I heard an attractive young woman say, "After a while I found I couldn't cope with the four children and all, and I needed drinks in the morning to keep me going. Then I was sipping through the day and having blackouts; I couldn't remember what my husband and I had talked about the night before. I was hiding my liquor in the coffeepot and medicine bottles in the bathroom so I could sneak there and drink when we had company.

"I rationalized that my husband was driving me to drink; when you're an alcoholic you can rationalize a thousand reasons for drinking. I was vomiting blood in the morning and passing out in the afternoon. Then eleven years ago I knew I had to stop and I joined AA, and I know now that I wasn't just a disgusting drunk. I know now that I was a very sick person."

From a strapping fifty-year-old executive I heard, "There are two things one should never forget about alcoholism: It's cunning and progressive. I was digging my own grave, drinking around the clock for five years. My wife divorced me. I remarried, got on the wagon for a year and was back on the stuff again—thirteen more years of stinking bouts, waking up in jails. I didn't have a shred of self-respect left, and I was an animal when I drank. Sixteen years ago I took my last drink and joined AA. I don't pray to God. I pray to my higher power. You figure *that* out!"

A chain-smoking matron stated, "I knew I had a drinking problem, but I wasn't ready to do anything about it. My husband traveled a lot, weeks at a time, and I needed liquor to tranquilize myself. It had all started innocently with a cocktail before dinner and became progressive, until I drank in the daytime for oblivion. I was sick of myself and wanted what others had. But I couldn't seem to find it until I found my higher power. I'm glad I'm an alcoholic because now there's a deeper meaning to my life and I can cope with it. But I do know, after what I've been through, that if I take another drink I'll probably die."

And from a Roman Catholic priest came the following: "I knew I was not sick because I drank but that I drank because I was sick. For six years, while drinking, I couldn't experience emotionally the person of Christ. I went through the motions as a priest, but I did not respond to the people. It reached a point when I couldn't even have soup without first drinking. But nineteen years ago I accepted my illness and joined AA. Today, when I get that insane urge for a drink, I make it a point to remember the last six months of my drinking and the first six months of my sobriety."

All this I heard and much of it I noted down, but I wasn't overly impressed. After all, *they* were alcoholics. *They* had done all those weird things. *They* had no willpower. *They* didn't know the meaning of discipline. I wasn't one of *them*.

Indeed, what impressed me most at those meetings was a poem read by one of the alcoholics who had brought copies of the doggerel to pass among his friends. I thought it was amusing and, after the meeting, paused at a bar to read it again:

> *The horse and mule live thirty years*
> *And nothing know of wines and beers.*
> *The goat and sheep at twenty die*
> *And never taste of scotch or rye.*
> *A cow drinks water by the ton*
> *And at eighteen is mostly done.*

The dog at fifteen cashes in
Without the aid of rum or gin.
The cat in milk or water soaks
And then in twelve short years it croaks.
The modest, sober bone-dry hen
Lays eggs for nogs, then dies at ten.
All animals are strictly dry;
They sinless live and swiftly die.
But sinful, ginful rum-soaked men
Survive for three-score years and ten;
And some of them, a very few,
Stay pickled till they're ninety-two.

Yes, I thought it was cute. I also thought it was very, very true.

FOUR

For a man convinced he was not an alcoholic, I was developing an odd liking for hospitals where alcoholics congregate.

There were ten of us around the table in the dining room of one of the largest hospitals in the Midwest: a college dean, the wife of a judge, an airline pilot, a Catholic priest who taught psychology, the wife of a warehouse owner, a tugboat captain, a plumber from Indiana, the statuesque wife of a magazine publisher, the owner of a shipyard and myself—quite an unusual assortment.

None of us had met before, but we had one thing in common: We were there because we had recently been drinking too much. This was not a psychiatric ward; it was a full-blown alcoholism unit within the hospital which had a four-week rehabilitation program.

Although I was befuddled that night after three weeks of fairly steady drinking, I have a good remembrance of some of my fellow diners:

I remember the tugboat captain, a tall Kentuckian in his late thirties, who had an infectious sense of humor. He would be dead in three months from the alcohol-and-pills sickness he had come here to conquer.

The priest would attempt suicide after leaving rehab, one day after phoning me that "life is coming down too hard on me to fight anymore." The wife of the warehouse owner would be asked to leave rehab midway through the twenty-eight-day program because she had smuggled in a bottle of vodka "to test myself."

The shipyard owner, a jet-setter from Texas, would ask me one night how long the flight was from Chicago to New York. The next morning he would walk out of rehab —leaving behind his clothes, his luggage, and his wife, who had moved to a nearby hotel—take a taxi to the airport and fly to the Bahamas to attend "a party I'd forgotten about." This, after telling me, "The doctors back home said if I drink just one more quart of whisky I'll die." He had only 30 percent of his liver left.

The plumber, too, would disappear, unable to accept the fact that he was an alcoholic and could never again take so much as a "social" drink. I missed him because he used to regale me with fantastic tales about his cat, which, he claimed, was a confirmed alcoholic (his favorite tonic— revolting, I thought—was scotch and milk, and he had hooked his cat on it).

And I can also recall the wife of the publishing tycoon, who was to ask me to spend our first weekend pass together in a nearby hotel. On the day of her departure, after she had spent twenty-five hundred dollars on rehabilitation, I asked her if she felt she was now a "recovering alcoholic." She threw back her head and laughed. "All this is a bunch of crap. I'll be drunk on the plane tonight."

I had checked into the rehab unit after a day of de-toxification on the medical floor of the hospital. Walking with me from the medical to the rehab unit was an attractive woman whose bluish-green and purple face looked like a rainbow gone mad. I assumed she had had an accident involving drunken driving. She said she had fallen down the stairs leading to her basement, where she was going to hide a new liquor supply consisting of two quarts of scotch. She lay there unconscious for an hour until her husband came home. She smiled through loosened teeth. "Would you believe it," she said proudly, "those two bottles—neither one broke."

I had been taken to rehab by a friend, a Chicago businessman and an alcoholic who had not had a drink in nine years. He talked me into it after a three-hour conversation, during which I still felt I could probably handle my problem alone. Drinking had become a fret, but I didn't feel that I had anything to "surrender." I was to find later that the toughest stumbling block to rehabilitation is the inability to accept alcoholism as an illness like cancer or tuberculosis.

While about 90 percent of the patients in this particular hospital were kept in rehab for four weeks, I was "held over" a fifth week because, I was told, I was "hard to probe into." Also, my guilt complex (I hated the waste of time that drinking involved) was severe.

All patients interacted with several counselors, but each had an individual counselor for private sessions. The one assigned to me was a recovered alcoholic, and I disliked him from the start.

He was sandpaper on my soul because I felt he was snobbish, even arrogant. This is significant because I tend to be something of a snob myself. Another counselor even told me, "You're aloof, you're standoffish, always by yourself reading. Why don't you mix with the others?" I said nothing, but the reason was that I felt I didn't belong with a bunch of weak-willed drunks. Ego, in many alcoholics, is master and mistress.

I didn't like the way my counselor would coldly eye a suffering woman in front of perhaps thirty others and snap, "What you're saying is a lot of bull. Who do you think you're kidding besides yourself?" I thought that he bordered on the cruel (self-pity is another defect of the alcoholic) and I considered asking for a change of counselor.

After the first week it began to dawn on me that what I considered arrogance was actually a no-nonsense honesty. The talk among veteran alcoholics was that no psychiatrist, no clergyman, not even a spouse can spot phoniness in an alcoholic as swiftly and accurately as another alcoholic.

Once, when the counselor was discussing my guilt, he asked, "What's your concept of God?" I replied, "Compassion."

"So you concede that God forgives you for what you think is some sort of sin of drinking?"

"Of course."

"But you won't forgive yourself. Who do you think you are—God?"

He had me boxed in and had penetrated my armor. Then and there I knew that not only could I not con him, but I didn't want to.

"It's changes in attitudes and thinking we look for," he explained. "When the alcoholic admits he's powerless over alcohol and doesn't like what he's doing, we come down hard on that motivation." At this point he was not talking to me the alcoholic but to me the curious journalist.

"Some con artists," he said, "want to stay here because the boss told them it's that or their job. That's baloney. The guy who comes here because his wife's on his back isn't going to make it either. The biggest problem here is their denial that there's a problem. Maybe the human animal can't get over his guilt, but you've got to get it to the level where you can at least like yourself. Otherwise you're ready to drink again.

"The men and women here are loaded with resentment, and that blocks what goes on here. You've got to want to stop drinking and want to do what's necessary to stop. Wanting to stop drinking and wanting to get out of trouble are two different things. Wanting to get over the hurt and wanting to cork the bottle are two different things."

The counselor sometimes would go two minutes without saying a word, possibly musing on what I supposed was his own drinking experience. "The good sign," he finally went on, "is when the alcoholic becomes selfish and says, 'I think I see what alcoholism is, and I want to be here for myself. If you want my boss to come in here and you want to talk to *him* privately, that's okay. If it takes your talking to my wife and kids, that's okay too.'"

The patients were encouraged to have employers and families participate in private group sessions. Many were repelled by the suggestion, but they were not pressured. Some of my children, in the presence of my estranged wife and myself, were asked individually, "Whom are you more concerned about, your mother or your father?"

In each case the answer was "mother." She evidently thought this meant they loved me more (which was neither the question nor the answer) and broke into tears. After the session I told the counselor, "What the hell did you do that for, you damned sadist?"

He pursed his lips and gave me a cold smile. "If she could put up with your drinking for years, she could put up with ten minutes of this." His logic hit me like a bucket of ice water; its meaning penetrated and the sting of it occasionally returns to this day.

I remained cynical about some of the methods used by the counselors, but at least they were impressive. No longer on medication (which usually ends after a week), I was seized with a sudden, powerful nervousness one morning. Hurrying to the day's first session, I stopped at the nurses' station and asked for a tranquilizer. It was denied me. No more than three minutes later the therapy session began with the head counselor telling the group, "We're worried about Paul." She explained the tranquilizer incident. I was stunned that the news had been relayed to the meeting so swiftly. "It's no big deal," I said. "You warned us that we'd go into a bad dip the third week, and I just felt shaky."

Counselor: "Don't you understand? You weren't just asking for a tranquilizer. You were reaching for a drink."

It happens that I have an obsessive fear of pills of any kind, and have never taken a tranquilizer or sleeping pill except when confined inside a hospital. "You're overdoing this," I said. "I never take pills! I just thought a tranquilizer would help me this morning. I was dropping and misplacing things for some reason."

Counselor: "You were nervous and wanted a tranquilizer. What'll happen when you leave here and run into a real crisis? It'll be like what just happened. You'll want to reach for a drink."

The counselor then asked the patients for their opinions. Most agreed with him. I felt foolish and angry.

A woman patient raised her hand to tell us that she had taken pills at home on her weekend pass. She was crying because she'd heard that she would be summarily sent home.

Another patient: "Give her another chance. She looked awful when she came in here. She looks in pretty good shape now."

Woman: "I'm so sorry. I don't want to go back to pills. I was afraid to go home for the weekend. I want to make it. I don't want to kill myself."

Counselor: "The group here is on your side, but I don't know if I'm sold on you. Maybe you need long-term care in a halfway house." Halfway houses are small, nonhospital institutions to which patients who have no family or should not yet be reunited with their families are recommended for further rehabilitation.

I later asked the head of the unit, a psychiatrist, about patients being asked their opinions in such cases. "We need to know," he explained, "how you feel about whether and when a patient should be sent home. But you are not responsible for the decision. That's in our hands. The process of the open discussion of a patient's problem is more important than the content."

Another female patient angrily said she didn't want her employer to become involved. The counselor snapped, "I think you don't figure you're an alcoholic. I don't know what you're doing here. I don't think you want to be helped. Maybe you think this is a good place for a vacation?"

Male voice from the back of the room: "You would think that, you bastard!"

Woman: "I can think of a hell of a lot better places for a vacation. I don't want to be here."

The consensus was that she was frightened and should be kept on. But she was recommended for early discharge and a stay in a halfway house.

I walked to the coffee room with a woman patient after the session. "I went home for the weekend," she said, "and the house was a mess. My counselor said if it's a mess next weekend, and I get worked up, to just leave and get back here. He says this is a selfish program and I've got to think only of myself now. So now I don't give a damn about the house and my husband. I don't want to die—so he can go screw himself!"

I discovered that, on the whole, women were much more distressed and frustrated about being in rehab than men. One woman, the wife of an ophthalmologist, told me at breakfast, "What am I doing here? My husband's a bisex-

ual. And he says he knows more about all this than all the
doctors here put together. He's ashamed I'm here. I know
if he had his way he'd come here with a bomb and blow
the fucking place up. He's got a problem, him and his god-
damned boyfriends, and I've got a problem, but he's out
there and I'm in here." Her husband never visited her during the four weeks she was in rehab, and shortly after being
discharged she filed for divorce.

I also found that in the vast majority of cases the alcoholic had some sort of marital-sexual problem before the
drinking began to take a serious turn.

When my first weekend pass came up (9 A.M. Saturday
to 8 P.M. Sunday), I told my counselor I didn't want to go
home. "It's not that I'm afraid I'll drink," I said. "But the
domestic situation's been bad for some time and, frankly, I
guess I want to stay in the womb." I thought he'd be
pleased I wanted to remain close to rehab care. He wasn't.
"You're copping out," he said. "You're afraid to face reality. You've got to go out into the world again a bit at a
time."

"What if I refuse to go?"

"It'll go down on your chart." He pursed his lips again.
"Go, and if it gets bad, get back here pronto."

When I came back about ten hours ahead of the dead-
line, he asked me how it had been. "It wasn't good," I said.
"The big thrill was getting a haircut. I caught up with the
bills."

"Think how high that pile of bills would be after four
weeks if you didn't go home," he said.

At one session the counselor wrote on the blackboard:
(1) I want to stop drinking. (2) I have to stop drinking.
He asked patients to make their selections. One woman
said, "I pick both Nos. 1 and 2."

Counselor: "You don't get an extra choice, kid. You

play all the angles. That's what you've been doing since you got here."

Most picked No. 2 for various reasons (bad health, social life ruined, "I'm no good to others," "I lost my driver's license and I'm scared").

Counselor: "No. 1 should be your choice. To *have* to stop is not the answer. You've got to *want* to stop. The reasons you gave are okay, but they're not good enough."

Male patient: "My wife loves me so much now that I'm here."

Counselor, unsmiling: "She loves you for the wrong reason. And I think you're here for the wrong reason."

A female patient started to explain her marital problems, but the counselor cut her short. "We're not interested in anybody's sexual problems here. You sound to me like you're pretty foxy, lady. You're always looking for loopholes."

Woman: "That means I'm smart."

Counselor: "No, it means you're sly."

The counselor later explained to me in private, "It's not that we're not interested in sex and marital problems. We are, but in the context of alcoholism's effects on sex. The immediate problem here is alcoholism, period. Once we get that straightened out, we can look into other problems. Of course we're concerned with 'sick' relationships between male and female alcoholics which are typical of the sick alcoholic. Such relationships don't occur here any more often than they occur among alcoholics on the outside."

One such relationship occurred while I was there. It involved a married male patient who had had three sexual interludes in rehab with a female patient. (Their trysting place was in the basement laundry room, for heaven's sake.) The woman, an out-of-town nurse, had told her counselor about it and was abashed that her newfound

lover wanted the sudden affair to end. The counselor
insisted that the matter be brought up for discussion at a
full group session.

It was one of the most embarrassing moments I have
ever experienced.

Here was a distraught, alcoholic nurse instructed to describe before a large group of strangers how and why she
had been fornicating in the laundry room with a married
man she had just met while both were hospitalized for rehabilitation. She even explained how, on one occasion,
they had used the ironing board, flattened out on the floor,
as their coital nest. (The patient next to me whispered,
"This is more fun than porno movies.")

The man, of course, was furious that the nurse had
blurted out the bargain-basement dalliance and enraged
that it had been brought up before the group without his
prior knowledge. The two even got into a heated argument
about her failure to use contraception, and the miserable
encounter developed into a shouting match over who had
suggested the idea in the first place.

As usual, the group was asked to comment. Never have I
seen so many people show such profound interest in their
shoes and the ceiling. I felt like having a drink. I suspect I
wasn't alone.

Later I challenged the chief counselor on the propriety
of publicly airing the couple's awkward passion in such clin-
ical detail. "We don't condone what happened," he said,
"but the problem is not the hanky-panky. The reason we
made a general discussion of it is that she's so broken up
over the end of the affair that she might go back to her
booze and pills when she leaves here. He's so worried about
his wife finding out, he could go back to the bottle, too. All
we're concerned with now is that they don't grab *any* excuse to take that first drink when they leave here. We con-

sider the team approach essential if the whole person is to be treated."

One real jolt came during a private discussion on the rehab's work and purpose, when the head of the unit told me:

"One half of the patients here now are going to make it. The other half won't. An emotionally critical period will occur for most of them ninety days after they leave here. Some of them will never weather it. After treatment here there are two thrusts. One must be directed at the drinking problem, and that's active participation in AA. But two thirds of the people here want nothing to do with AA. They feel they can do it on their own. This is sad when you realize that with AA after discharge the success rate is 65 percent. With AA plus a second thrust (outpatient treatment, family counseling, psychiatry, halfway house and so forth) the ratio jumps to 81 percent.

"There's family counseling when needed. Others need to return here every week for outpatient therapy. I would recommend psychiatry to the patient who thinks he needs it only if he goes for one of the other thrusts as well, and if the psychiatrist will have him do something about his drinking rather than just treating the symptoms. If he's only digging up your past, that's dangerous because often he's only ticking off a bunch of reasons why you *should* drink."

But the worst jolt was yet to come.

On my last day in rehab we had a session on resentments, and I had occasion to mention that the thought of my daughters using my razor to shave their legs irritated the life out of me. A few weeks later, relaxing at home, I received a gift. It was the most expensive razor on the market. It came from the tugboat captain with whom I had shared gallons of coffee and hours of fun conversation.

A few days after I sent him a note of thanks, he was dead. He had hanged himself in his room.

Some mornings, while I am shaving, his face and his laughter come back to me. And so does the thought of what his illness did to him.

FIVE

Funny things happen to alcoholics on their way to sobriety, but in retrospect the scenario that follows had all the hilarity of a ruptured spleen. It triggered off something in my head that sent me back to swigging, perhaps because it was so chaotic, even disastrous. What made it deplorable was some inept judgments on my part, and while others had angered me, I was really angry at myself.

The farce dated back about three years, when a New York individual, who described himself as a playwright and former Hollywood actor, came to see me in Chicago to engage my writing services. I had then been enjoying a yearlong period of sobriety. He wondered if I would "doctor" a musical play he had written. He also described himself as a confidant of Broadway producers, a part owner of bowling alleys, a friend of moneyed (if vague) people and a composer. He showed me some of his compositions from his portfolio, but since I don't read music I took his word for it. Unfortunately, I took his word for everything else.

He explained that he was familiar with my column (which was syndicated) and had read all my books. This was credible, because one night in a posh Chicago restaurant, after singing a pair of his songs to me (ruining the appetite of nearby diners), he rattled off the plots of my books with accuracy.

It's embarrassing, in this age of gay abandon, to have a man croon to you over cooling cutlets and under the gaze of a puzzled maître d', but my ego was piqued—a common syndrome among alcoholics. I did not ask him why he had not chosen any of hundreds of writers in New York, perhaps because I wanted to savor the honor of his flying all that distance to single me out to redo his play. I was sensitive to such things at the time because I was living the single life—no longer with a wife and away from the children —and loneliness makes strange billows in the dark clouds of the mind. But while I was flattered, I told him I wanted time to think it over. I had doubts. Did I really want to return to Manhattan, where former friends and temptations clustered? Would I be happy far away from the children? Would I be safe away from AA friends I had come to like and respect?

Months passed and my New York friend returned a few times to Chicago, where we discussed his proposition over and over again. He also wrote and phoned occasionally, suggesting it was time I collected my guts and brought them East.

Finally, in a period of funk (I had left the newspaper and free-lance writing was slow) I succumbed. He was difficult to pin down on financial details, but on the surface I sensed a challenge. I wanted to get moving again, earn money and show my children that I could again conquer New York.

I must say he was a sincere, charming rascal, in no sense a con man. Though about sixty, he was as exuberant as a schoolboy at recess and gifted with gab. He described a large, beautiful apartment not far from the glamor of Madison Avenue where I would live with him, and this sanctum would, of course, include my own rent-free "studio."

Then the curtain rose on the comedy of errors.

Confident that I would be in New York for some time, I had packed and shipped two big trunks. The absurdity was that he had given me the address of his former wife; that's where the trunks were heading, and I never did see them in the short time I was in New York. They contained just about everything I owned except some shirts, deodorant and a copy of *Abie's Irish Rose*, which I had thoughtfully brought in a traveling bag.

Upon arrival, I phoned to learn that the apartment was "not quite ready" and I would have to stay in a hotel that night. The money was already starting to dwindle, but I had no choice. My friend ("Blarney" from now on) picked me up the next day and took me to his apartment, where I found (1) a pretty young woman he was shacked up with; (2) her six-year-old daughter; (3) a minimum of furniture (none in my "studio"); (4) abundant amounts of litter; (5) no drapes or curtains; (6) two beds that apparently hadn't been made since Simmons turned them out and (7) a closetful of hideous lollipops (about which more later). I'm almost certain there were more ice cubes in the refrigerator than food.

It turned out that Blarney and his paramour were barely on speaking terms, except when snarling at each other; it was plain that my arrival was one of the reasons. He was "inviting" her and her daughter to leave the premises by the end of the month to make room, he told her, for this bigshot writer from Chicago who was going to put him on Broadway. What he told me that first night was that he was throwing her out because another lady whose charms he preferred was waiting in the wings to move in. I felt about as welcome as a piranha in the swimming pool.

The two beds were occupied by Blarney and his mistress, but they slept in separate bedrooms. ("No sex," he

confided. "It never did work out.") The third bedroom
belonged to the little girl, who was directed to move into
her mother's bedroom, and her room—presto—became my
"studio."

The easiest way to describe my "studio" is to say that it
wasn't.

To begin with, it had no bed, although there was a plain
mattress on the floor. But the mattress had no linen; it
even lacked the dignity of a pillow, so Blarney cheerfully
provided a rolled-up blanket. Determined not to lose my
cool, not to mention my medulla oblongata, I found a
thick Sunday edition of the New York *Times* in the
kitchen, inserted it beneath the rolled-up blanket, and had
myself a headrest. But it happens that I have three mal-
functioning disks at the back of the neck, so I spent that
night reading the New York *Times*.

I couldn't read sitting up because there was no chair in
the room, and the desk on which I was to rewrite Blarney's
play was no wider than an orange crate and about as high
as a telephone table. It was fine for the child's schoolwork,
but it would barely have accommodated a typewriter.
There wasn't even a coat hanger on which to suspend my
clothes.

So there I was—shaving kit, shirts, shorts, wallet and my
one traveling suit laid out on the floor across the sports sec-
tion of the New York *Times*—surrounded by the child's
school books, toys, sneakers, piles of little-girl para-
phernalia and her entire wardrobe—all on the floor.

While Blarney's girl friend spoke to me only with her
eyes—and it was pretty baleful conversation—her bewildered daughter took a liking to me. Too much, in fact. She
had the disconcerting habit of popping into my "studio" at
various times, unannounced, in quest of clothes, books or
toys. Her greeting was always "whatcha doin'?" Once, as I

was struggling, naked, into my shorts, she barged in with the interesting question, "Whatcha doin'?" I felt like saying, "With no curtains on the windows, little girl, I'm standing here praying that your neighbors don't call the police."

Since my trunks were lost somewhere and I had no typewriter, no work material of any kind, there were times of long nothingness. I was looking out the window one morning before she had left for school, envying the sun because it, at least, had something to do, when she came in and asked again, "Whatcha doin'?" Sadly I looked back at her and said, "I don't know, honey, I really don't know."

The general idea was that I was to have the use of those elegant diggings for two purposes—to help Blarney put his two plays in order and to write my own works, notably a book I owed my publisher. This arrangement partly explains why there had been little discussion of a fee for my services.

Then came two successive shocks. Blarney was aware that one of my previous books (*A Pennant for the Kremlin*) was under consideration as a musical by a well-known producer. He let me have it:

"One reason I'm glad you're here is your contacts. I want you to introduce him to me and get him to have me write the music for your Pennant play when it gets into production."

The producer in question was in Hollywood at the time, so I mumbled something about giving it some thought. The truth was, I could not suggest to the producer that Blarney be given a crack at the music because, while I could not judge his talent in that area, I had read his lyrics. My verdict there was that they were destined for merciful oblivion.

To put it gently, the script did not have the stuff to hold up as a high school production.

"There isn't one sympathetic character in the play," I told Blarney, pointing out that the play would have to be rebuilt from the opening curtain, and the heroine, in particular, would have to be reconstructed from the neck up. He agreed reluctantly, but only in small part, and then went on to the second shock.

It seemed that some years earlier he and a friend had developed a brand of lollipop shaped in the likeness of characters from the onetime monster craze among children. A large candy firm had come out with the same idea and the two outfits were at legal loggerheads as to which one had thought of the fright suckers first.

Blarney was aware of my friendship with several prominent New York attorneys, and he asked if I would go see them and convince one of them to take on his lollipop litigation.

So here we were with the contacts again. Out of that "studio" I was to get involved with busy attorneys and million-dollar lawsuits, get him to connect with an influential Broadway producer, rewrite his plays, try to stay out of the way of the new shack-up arrangement and, when there was time to spare, perhaps work on my book.

I was not only becoming disillusioned, I was becoming angry and even a little scared.

Meanwhile, since my working tools—notes, research material, typewriter, copy paper and the rest—were still lost in transit somewhere, I was doing little but sitting on that insufferable mattress, reading legal correspondence on the war of the lollipops.

I suppose the final disillusionment came after I noticed that Blarney would leave the apartment each morning and stay away until sunset, when he would return with his dinner—sandwiches picked up at a nearby delicatessen. One night I said, "Where do you go all day?"

"Well," he replied, "there's not much money coming in right now, so I'm looking for a job."

I was aghast. He had told me about an elderly million-airess standing by, waiting for me to write "only four scenes" (with music) if ever we could find time to get together on them.

"Then," he said, "I'll get a small cast and she wants to audition the scenes."

He saw my face fall. "But don't worry," he gushed, "she's got millions and she doesn't care how she spends it, and we'll probably make a lot on the lollipop thing, and maybe your Kremlin thing will go as a play and maybe a movie. Hey, we've got it made! Don't worry about a thing."

Now that I think of it, that was not the last straw. That came one morning, a week after I'd arrived, when I was alone in the apartment taking a bath. There wasn't a bar of soap to be found anywhere. There must have been a dozen jars and bottles and spray cans on the side of the tub and in the medicine cabinet, but no soap.

I was determined to create some suds because now I was angry, angry enough to do anything stupid. I emptied everything I could find into the water. If it's in the bathroom and it has to do with the body and cleansing, I figured, it'll work out.

I sat there, splashing away, when it suddenly struck me. Oh, no, I thought. I think I'm bathing in her douche! I wanted to cry. In fact, I think I did a little. Either that or some of that douche got into my eyes.

An hour later, dressed and smelling a bit strange, I sat again on that ridiculous mattress, and it slowly dawned on me: My God! I thought, what am I doing here? Is this conquering New York?

I don't know why, but I took a slow walk to the closet where the lollipops were stored. I stood for a long minute staring at the stacks of the hideous stuff. Then I went to the telephone and long-distanced Georgia, my daughter, with whom I'd been staying near Chicago. "Just promise you won't laugh at me," I said. She promised, and I gave her a quick rundown on how I'd taken New York by storm.

She said just one thing. "Dad, come home. Now!"

I told her to call the van people and have them reroute my trunks back to Chicago. I collected my belongings off the floor in the "studio" and a few hours later I left for Chicago—but not before buying a bar of soap.

Unfortunately, there was more than soap to pick up. I had to have a traveling companion. It was a bottle of vodka.

For many an alcoholic, a funny thing may happen to him on his way to sobriety. It's called relapse. But it's not really *that* funny.

Relapse is what kept sending me back to hospitals. Too often relapse is what sends the alcoholic to his grave.

SIX

There were to be a dreadful number of relapses, and one day one of them brought me to the Hinsdale Sanitarium and Hospital. It is a Seventh-Day Adventist, 440-bed general hospital in Hinsdale, Illinois, an attractive, partly pastoral suburb twenty miles west of Chicago. (I didn't have far to go because Hinsdale was where I had bought a home when I came to work in Chicago.)

The seventy-five-year-old "San," as the hospital is popularly called, is the only hospital I shall identify by name. It is the place which gave me the incentive to finally do something about my problem. Nothing but nice things happened to me the many times I was there, and the kindness and efficiency of its Seventh-Day Adventist staff are something that beggars description. Some unpleasant things occurred in other hospitals, but it would be pointless to embarrass them because of the ineptitude—and even stupidity—of some staff members.

Example: In one hospital with an alcoholic rehab unit, I opened the refrigerator where soft drinks and juices were kept for the patients. Poking around for a 7 Up, I came up with a can of beer. I wasn't thirsting for a beer, but I was curious; I looked in and found two more cans of beer.

The head nurse happened by as I stood there with the beer in my hand and I made some remark about the nice change in medication. She was horrified. It turned out that one of the nurses was fond of soothing the monotony of the night shift with beer and decided that the refrigerator was the obvious place to store her brew.

Example: In another hospital I was present when a nurse made a mistake that could have been dangerous. It was weekend-pass time, and the patients going home for a day or two were given medication (usually Valium or Librium and vitamins) to take with them. It was given to us in little brown envelopes that contained instructions on when and how many to take.

A few hours after reaching home, one patient opened his envelope to find a large assortment of pills and capsules with which he was unfamiliar. He had the precautionary presence of mind to call the nurses' station. Again the nurse in charge was appalled. The envelope he had was meant for another alcoholic who was also an epileptic and had a moribund liver.

The two men had been given the wrong envelopes. I don't know what might have happened had they followed instructions, but I do know that the seriously sick one was called immediately and ordered to return to the hospital at once.

Worse things (worse because they happened to me) occurred in other hospitals, and they will be related later under the rubric of "hospitals anonymous."

It was at the San that I first met Dr. Charles L. Anderson, chairman of the hospital's department of psychiatry, a gentle, soft-spoken man with a weakness for loud shirts and huge bow ties. He laughed with his eyes, and his face reminded me of the friendly general store keeper so well depicted in Norman Rockwell's paintings. He took a liking to me and we found we shared an interest in reading, history and Scrabble.

Now in his early sixties, Dr. Anderson has been working in the field of alcoholism since 1941. He is widely known as an authority on the subject, although he doesn't know the taste of liquor. He serves on various alcoholism commissions and committees, and I think that what helped attract me to him was something he said shortly after we met:

"I could be an alcoholic. I don't know. And the only reason I don't know is that I've never taken a drink. But it's impossible for anyone, psychiatrist or whoever, to predict who will and will not be an alcoholic by means of personality tests and profiles and things like that.

"We find certain neurotic traits in a budding alcoholic, but then we find those same traits in other persons who have emotional problems but who are not alcoholics.

"I could go to a party tonight, take a few drinks, try it again next week and suddenly discover that I'm an alcoholic. It's still a mystery to medical science, and the only thing we're really sure of is that alcoholism only happens to people who drink. This is facetious, of course, but it's the only hard answer we have for now."

Toward the end of one of our conversations, Dr. Anderson said, "I have a friend, a doctor, who's an alcoholic. Would you talk with him if I ask him to stop by?"

I really didn't feel like talking with any alcoholic, but I was intrigued by the idea of an alcoholic doctor. To me that was not possible, no more than an armless barber. But out of curiosity, and because Dr. Anderson exuded a feeling of trust, I told him I would talk with his colleague.

The next evening, Dr. Mike, a dapper, good-looking man in his late forties, came to my room. With him was Jim, about the same age, a tall, stern-faced businessman who looked as if he had come to give me a scolding. He didn't; the scoldings were to come later. Also to come later was the growth of a relationship which was to make him, to this day, a close friend.

That first meeting was a surprise. They did not probe or pontificate. They merely talked about themselves as recovered alcoholics—what it was like when they drank, what happened when they stopped and what it was like now.

I couldn't conceal my astonishment. "A doctor and an insurance executive—alcoholics!" I exclaimed. "I usually associate alcoholics with skid row."

"Skid row?" Dr. Mike laughed. "I've been on skid row without leaving home. Skid row can be your living room or it can be between your ears. That's what it was for me."

Jim interrupted. "Passing out on a two-inch carpet or in the gutter is the same thing; I've done it many times. You're equally close to the ground in both cases."

"Forget that skid row stuff," Dr. Mike went on. "It's a stigma. What would you say if I told you that only 4 percent of the people on skid row are alcoholics?"

"I'd say that's a figure you picked off the top of your head."

"It's a figure I picked out of official Washington, D.C., government reports. Ninety-five percent of the bums on skid row are not alcoholics. Think about that."

I looked at Dr. Mike. "How bad did it get for you?" I asked.

He brought his thumb and forefinger together: "I came this close to being kicked out of the medical society. Some doctor friends saved my fanny. I'll tell you how bad it was. Once I delivered twins and the nurse kept saying she thought it might be triplets. I was foggy, of course, and I said, 'When I say a woman's going to have twins, she has twins!' So I delivered the twins and went to the lounge for a smoke. A few minutes later the nurse came into the lounge and told me that a third baby had just popped out."

I nodded in disbelief. "I was as sneaky as they come," Dr. Mike went on. "I couldn't bear to let my family see me drink, but I'd exhausted all the hiding places, at home and at the office, so I was down to hiding vodka under the hood of my car, in the plastic container, you know, that holds the solvent to wipe the windshield. At night I'd go to the garage and suck it out with a rubber tube. Sometimes, while on a drive with my wife, I'd tell her I thought the engine sounded funny and I'd pull over to the side of some lonely road, lift up the hood, pull out my rubber tube and get down a couple of belts."

I asked Jim how bad it had been for him. "Well," he sighed, lighting a cigar, "I lost a few jobs, my first wife divorced me, I can't count the times I was thrown in jail and once I was just about pronounced dead on the spot after a real bad alcoholic convulsion. How's that for starters?"

After a while Jim and Mike told me about their respective recoveries through AA. They asked if I'd go with them to a meeting that night. "I feel awful," I stammered, "and I . . ."

"You don't look bad; you look pretty good for a guy who's been drinking for two weeks," Jim lied. "Dr. Anderson okayed a pass. We'll pick you up at eight."

That night they took me to a meeting in the basement of a school. It was impossible to avoid reading AA's famed Twelve Steps, conceived by AA founders Bill Wilson and Dr. Bob Smith, which hung in a gigantic frame affixed to the wall:

1. We admitted we were powerless over alcohol—that our lives had become unmanageable.

2. Came to believe that a Power greater than ourselves could restore us to sanity.

3. Made a decision to turn our will and our lives over to the care of God—*as we understood Him.*

4. Made a searching and fearless moral inventory of ourselves.

5. Admitted to God, to ourselves and to another human being the exact nature of our wrongs.

6. Were entirely ready to have God remove all these defects of character.

7. Humbly asked Him to remove our shortcomings.

8. Made a list of all persons we had harmed and became willing to make amends to them all.

9. Made direct amends to such people wherever possible, except when to do so would injure them or others.

10. Continued to take personal inventory and, when we were wrong, promptly admitted it.

11. Sought through prayer and meditation to improve our conscious contact with God *as we understood Him,* praying only for knowledge of His will for us and the power to carry that out.

12. Having had a spiritual awakening as the result of these steps, we tried to carry this message to alcoholics, and practice these principles in all our affairs.

I went to meetings for several nights, during which the discussions were mostly about the Twelve Steps and one repeated admonition: "Don't take that first drink." But my mind was elsewhere, mostly on me. How could I be an alcoholic? Why, I used to boast (and it was generally true) that I never had hangovers, and my hangover cure was simple: "First you squeeze the juice from a quart of vodka . . ."

But me an alcoholic? Incredible. Sure, Jim was an executive and Mike was a doctor and they were alcoholics, but they did not have my family environment and breeding,

**Please Retain This
Receipt To Ensure
A Prompt Refund
Or Exchange.**

$$\frac{\begin{array}{r}350\\4\end{array}}{1400}$$

**Please Retain This
Receipt To Ensure
A Prompt Refund**

HILLS DEPARTMENT STORES
FAMOUS FOR LOW PRICES EVERY DAY
KOKOMO IND.

STORE #0042   REG. 003   OPR 10
4700427887   VIDEO TAPE

         IN 5% TAX(1)

              TOTAL

CASH   10.25

         CHANGE

    THANK YOU FOR SHOPPING HILLS
      9/21/98   6:45PM   0248

------SAVE BOTTOM PORTION FOR------

HILLS 4SUPPLY-A-SCHOOL PROGRAM

STORE #0042   9/21/98   TOTAL
OPR 10   0248

and a man with my lineage and background just could not be an alcoholic.

I was born in Canada of warm cordial parents and had a happy childhood braced by love. My mother (Marie Dubuc) was French Canadian, the daughter of Sir Joseph Dubuc, Chief Justice of Manitoba, knighted by King George V and honored by the Pope, whose career was great enough to warrant two biographies. I certainly was the only kid on the block whose grandmother was addressed as "Lady," not "Mrs." My father, of Irish parentage, was a mathematics professor elected to the Manitoba legislature. My mother had five brothers; one was Chief Justice of Alberta, one was a doctor and the other three were lawyers. My father's dad was a D.L.S. (Dominion Land Surveyor) and his brother, Jack, was a lifelong senator in Ottawa. The family entourage consisted of judges, lawyers, doctors, company presidents, a priest, and an ambassador to Belgium. And there wasn't a boozer in the bunch.

I had three brothers. One was a mine superintendent, another a buyer for an aircraft company and the third, Vincent, owns a catering firm. I have two sisters. Of the five, the score was: three abstainers and two social drinkers. Hardly the backdrop for a slave to the sauce.

Then there was the matter of education. My father did not speak French (my mother was bilingual) and wanted me to have the benefits of a bilingual education. First he sent me to a French-language Jesuit college for five years, the main feature of which was a massive dose of Latin and Greek, and then to an English-language Jesuit college for another four years.

During those AA meetings I kept thinking, "How, from such surroundings, could I be the alcoholic black sheep of the family? And if, in fact, I were, why?" It didn't make sense. I would never have had the time to become an alcoholic anyway. I had gone from newspaper reporter to Western Canada superintendent for United Press International, an editor at *Time* magazine in New York, syndicated columnist, had written several books on the side, and had raised eight children.

I wanted to tell this to Jim and Mike during those first meetings, but I was too nervous and unsure. Anyway, better to be thought a "problem drinker" than a pedigreed blowhard.

One night, as Dr. Mike was driving me back to the hospital from a meeting, I asked him why he and Jim had come to see me. "Well," he said, "I guess it was the way Dr. Anderson put it when he called us. He said, 'There's a man here who, I think, should be salvaged.'"

I felt I had to apologize to Dr. Mike. "You have to be at your hospital at seven each morning, and here you're spending your nights driving me around. I feel awful."

"It makes me feel good," he said. "You think I'm doing this just for you? Hell, I'm doing it for me. Remember what it says in that twelfth step, about carrying the message to others? That's all I'm doing. And I've got to do it to stay sober."

I had heard almost those same words before. And I was to hear them again and again.

But it wasn't that twelfth step that stayed with me after those meetings. It was a couple of "drunk" stories (alcoholics have an endless supply) based on two other steps. I took a liking to the alcoholic who stopped two men on the street and said to one:

"You don't know me, but I have to tell you something. I've just joined AA and they tell me I have to make amends to people I've harmed. Well, for the past two years I've been sleeping with your wife. I'm sorry. I'll make amends. I hope you'll forgive me, and it'll never happen again."

With that the alcoholic turned on his heels and walked away. The man he had addressed turned to his friend and said, "How do you like that guy? He sobers up and now my wife ain't good enough for him."

The other story involved the drunk who went from his first AA meeting to a bar and ordered six manhattans. After they were lined up, he told the bartender, "Now throw that first one down the sink." The bartender did as he was instructed, but the look of puzzlement was clearly evident on his face. The drunk explained:

"You see, I've joined AA and they tell me to always remember one thing: Don't take that first drink."

That's how much of an impression AA had made on me that week.

SEVEN

Midway through my very first drink—I was nineteen years old at the time—I knew I had found a new friend. I assumed we would just remain friends; there was no warning that I would let that drink become my mistress instead.

Some authorities on alcoholism claim that if an individual can remember his first drinking experience—not his first drunk—chances are he is probably an alcoholic. Others theorize that some sufferers do not become alcoholics, but that alcoholics are born and not made, hooked from the first tilt of the bottle, "instant alcoholics" not necessarily the victims of the controversial heredity factor.

I know I am in the first category and I am almost convinced I belong in the second—an "instant alcoholic" not cursed by the heredity factor.

The remembrance of my first drinking experience is so clear it is eerie. Not only do I remember the name of the hotel where it happened, I recall the name of the street on which the hotel stood, the names of at least three of the youths who were with me at the time, and that it was an extremely cold January night. Also clear in my mind is the fact that cold beer on a cold night seemed to be a stupid idea.

At both colleges I attended I went in for hockey and boxing, and when the northern Quebec gold-and-copper mine where my brother worked needed boxers and hockey players for the company team, he sent for me. Once I became a company athlete, I became part of the "special people"; we stood out from the others and were given the undeserved status of "stars" in the small mining communities. It was neither proper nor ethical, since amateurs were not paid, but we wore clothes that we normally could not afford—a gift of the company. We "worked" four or five hours at the mine instead of eight because the team had to have time to train, and when an athlete got into trouble with bills, that was often taken care of quietly by the company. We were the imported "heroes," brought in to make the company look good, who traveled to neighboring Quebec towns to do battle in the ring or on the ice with the imported "heroes" of other company towns. And when we returned, there was often a little beer drinking on the bus ride home. At first I ignored the beer (I'd never had a drink in all my college days), but one night after a hockey game the bus broke down before departure and the team whiled away the time in a hotel where there was beer. That was when I had my first one. It tasted strange, but it gave me a good feeling.

After a couple of months of this I noticed that beer was no longer a casual post-game ritual; I began to look forward to the ride home because the beer provoked laughter and fellowship. Yet I recall wondering, now and then, why the beer suddenly had become important. This was long ago, but I remember that at this early point my reaction to those drinks was different from that of my teammates. Today I believe that some combination of psychological, physical and cultural experiences produced an unusual, different response to that first drink—that I was an "instant alcoholic." After about a year I was getting mildly sloshed on payday (didn't all miners get drunk on payday?). One payday I made a semisodden decision that was probably my finest while under the influence.

For a long time I had admired a typewriter in the window of a secondhand store. There had always lurked in me the thought that I would some day be a writer. Whenever I passed that window, the typewriter seemed to be staring at me, almost beckoning. Well fortified, I strolled into the store one day and bought it. It was a move that paid off; I wrote mining-area articles for Quebec newspapers and magazines, and this won me a job as a reporter in Montreal. I threw myself joyfully into this new career and put the beer aside—not, unfortunately, for noble reasons, but because the hard stuff did what I expected more quickly, and because there was so much of it being given away in Montreal that there was barely any need to buy it. I have seldom touched beer since.

After a few weeks on the inside writing obituaries, the newspaper sent me out on my first "beat," the Criminal Courts Building, where I covered the daily drama of trials ranging from prostitution to murder. It was exciting; seeing my first few bylines in the paper touched my ego much as it was stirred in the earlier, dinky-hero days in the mines.

I soon discovered that French-Canadian lawyers were generous types, especially when their names appeared in newspaper accounts of the trials in which they pleaded. They would march into the court building's crowded press room (there were eight dailies in Montreal at the time) with bottles of liquor "in appreciation" of the reporters' handling of cases that involved them. If they'd had a good day or won a case, they'd come in with a quart or two, drink a toast to their triumph, and leave the bottles behind.

Our press room sometimes looked like a free bar; there was whoopee water galore and we drank it straight, out of paper cups. It was not unusual, at the end of the day, for a judge or other court officials to drop in for a quick one on the way home. Reporters, too, were "special people"; it was all quite jolly and I knew that being a newspaperman was going to be ruddy good fun.

But why the continued interest in drink? Why was I unknowingly letting it take hold of me? I suppose I will never really know, but it leads to the obvious questions: What is alcoholism? Who is an alcoholic?

There are varying definitions. The National Council on Alcoholism and the American Medical Society on Alcoholism call it a "chronic, progressive and potentially fatal disease characterized by tolerance, physical dependency and pathological organ changes, all of which are the direct or indirect consequences of the alcohol ingested."*

According to Dr. Daniel J. Anderson, president of the Hazelden Foundation treatment center in Minnesota, "Alcoholism can best be described as a behavioral disorder, one in which certain chronic and progressive phenomena take place in certain rather well-defined stages. Although there are many definitions of alcoholism, they all share certain elements: excessive drinking, exaggerated dependency on alcohol, preoccupation with drinking, surreptitious drinking, loss of control over the amount consumed or the time of drinking, and the obvious fact that even though the alcoholic has been in trouble on numerous occasions

* This definition comes from a joint statement of the National Council on Alcoholism and the American Medical Society on Alcoholism, as stated. See also the definition given by the American Medical Association in 1956, as well as this definition from the World Health Organization: "Alcoholics are those excessive drinkers whose dependence upon alcohol has attained such a degree that it shows a noticeable mental disturbance or an interference with their bodily or mental health, their interpersonal relationships and their smooth social and economic functioning, or shows the prodromal signs of such development" (from the Doubleday book *Drink*, by Constantine Fitz-Gibbon, p. 99).

over drinking, he still continues to drink. Such behavior suggests that alcoholism is far more than a symptom of some other underlying condition; that it is, rather, an illness in its own right."

The Rutgers University Center on Alcohol Studies is more succinct: "An alcoholic is one who is unable consistently to choose whether he shall drink or not and, if he drinks, is unable consistently to choose whether he shall stop or not."

There is a lessening of disagreement on the definition. It's significant that alcoholism has been officially recognized as a disease by the World Health Organization, the Public Health Department of the U. S. Government, the American Medical Association, the American Hospital Association, the American Psychiatric Association, the American Bar Association, and by every state government in the Union. It is also medically categorized as incurable but treatable, and can therefore be controlled.

Whether or not one agrees that it is a disease, it appears that alcoholism is assuming the proportions of an epidemic. At least it's clear to me that if alcoholism were a communicable disease, a state of national emergency would be declared. A study by the former Department of Health, Education, and Welfare's National Institute on Alcohol Abuse and Alcoholism (NIAAA) has declared that, after heart disease and cancer, alcoholism is the nation's most serious health problem.

The NIAAA also reported that in half of all murders committed in the United States, the killer, the victim, or both had been drinking; one fourth of all suicides were found to have significant amounts of alcohol in the blood; half of the 55,500 traffic deaths each year and 68 percent of the one million major injuries suffered in car accidents can be traced directly to a driver or pedestrian under the influence; alcohol abusers are seven times more likely to be separated or divorced than is the general population; and the cost of alcoholism is now rated at fifteen billion dollars a year in lost work time and accidents.

Earlier I used the word epidemic. The present estimate claims that there are fifteen million alcoholics in the United States (nearly half of them women), and their numbers increase by about one hundred thousand a year. It is also a fact that every alcoholic affects at least four persons close to him or her—the spouse, the employer, children, and so forth. Thus, we are dealing with an illness that is currently affecting, on a day-to-day basis, at least seventy-five million people in this country alone.

What kind of a person is the alcoholic? Dr. Ruth Fox, medical director of the National Council on Alcoholism, smashes many a myth with the following observation: "Most persons suffering from alcoholism are found in homes, offices, places of business and in every walk of life. The disease attacks without regard to social standing, occupation, intelligence, education, national origin, color or race. A small percentage have an underlying psychosis and many have a personality disturbance. However, many are not noticeably different from the rest of us except in their addiction to alcohol. Alcoholics after recovery generally prove to be gifted, talented, generous, responsible and idealistic people, as well as good parents and citizens."

When all is said and done, questioned, researched and reexamined, the unpleasant reality is that medical science and all the experts on alcoholism cannot produce a concrete, definitive answer to the questions: Who is an alcoholic and who is merely a problem drinker? What, precisely, causes alcoholism?

Quantity is not the ultimate factor, only a criterion. "We see people," says Harold Swift of the Hazelden Foundation, "who drink less than half a pint a day who are dying. Yet we see men who go through better than a fifth a day and still function well." Nor is the type of spirits an important factor; I know dozens of recovering alcoholics who reached the gutter without having taken anything but beer or wine. Most beers contain about 4.5 percent alcohol by volume. Fortified wines (sherry and port) contain 18 to 21 percent alcohol. Spirits are about 86 proof, which is stronger than 4.5 and 21 percent, but proof is just a trade method of stating alcoholic content and is exactly twice the alcohol strength. So 86-proof liquor contains 43 percent alcohol by volume. While this makes beer and wine seem less strong, it should be remembered that wine is usually taken in 4-ounce glasses and beer in 10-ounce mugs. Taken straight, spirits are usually drunk from 1.5-ounce shot glasses. So it takes only 1.25 glasses of wine or 1.5 mugs of beer to equal the alcohol in a shot of 86-proof liquor.

Behavioral scientist Don Calahan of the University of California prefers not to make fine distinctions. He insists that drinking is a continuum and that no fine line can be drawn between the heavy imbiber and the alcoholic: "The issue is why some people apparently waste their lives on alcohol while others don't. What's the 'glue' that binds some people to their alcohol problems?"

Mrs. Marty Mann, who founded the National Council on Alcoholism and who strongly affirmed that alcoholism is a disease, had an interesting no-nonsense view: "No one has ever found the way to turn a nonalcoholic into an alcoholic. There is a basic difference in people."

The treatment program at the Hinsdale San is based on that developed by Vernon E. Johnson, founder of the nonprofit Johnson Alcoholism Institute in Minneapolis. Johnson sums up the alcoholic problem in his book *I'll Quit*

Tomorrow: "Who contracts this illness? The answer seems to be that, mysteriously, all sorts of personalities become alcoholic. The difficult question is why some people cannot become alcoholic no matter how hard they try. A drinker has to be able to develop a tolerance for ethyl alcohol or he can't make it. If alcohol makes him sick and he throws up, he is immune.

"People of every stripe of character and morality become alcoholics, but ultimately the disease causes all its victims to behave in a destructive and antisocial way. In searching for common denominators, we have observed that the alcoholic is likely to be an achiever in his peer group. Interestingly, people who appear entirely phlegmatic seem less likely to become addicted to alcohol or other mood-changing chemicals. They just live along, and the frustrations of life don't seem to get to them; neither does alcohol. Another way of avoiding this conflict is not to care. Sociopaths appear to lack the values or conscience essential to the conflict we observe in alcoholics. They actually feel no shame.

"A misconception about alcoholism causes people to be fearful to confront alcoholics. We are told that the alcoholism may be a cover for some more serious emotional disorder, and that alcoholics can be shattered if they are cornered. Another misconception is that since he behaves the way he does, the alcoholic is heedless and does not care what damage his behavior causes. This leads to the erroneous assumption that he will be unresponsive to any attempts to help him. Because of his wide mood swings, the alcoholic is a formidable person to confront, and it is true that he is able skillfully to rationalize his own behavior. But he does not smash so easily, and there is an explanation for his careless behavior. Actually, he is loaded with self-hatred which is repressed and unconscious, and he projects this onto the persons around him.

"The people around an alcoholic do not realize how little he knows of himself and his behavior. He is not confronted by his own actions; many of them he is not even aware of, although those around him assume that he is. They believe that he sees himself as they see him. In point of fact, as the disease runs its course, he is increasingly deluded. He lives with increasing impairment of judgment, and eventually loses touch with his emotions entirely. He has conscious and unconscious ways of forgetting painful experiences. It is a matter of self-survival. If a person is alcoholic, by definition he is unable to recognize the fact. Any attempt to interrupt his drinking or change his life style he views as meddling."

The alcoholic resents the "meddling" because everywhere he goes, everywhere he looks he sees drinking as the proper thing to do, as a way of life, as a perfectly natural social encounter. Temptations, like taverns and liquor stores, are everywhere: the martini lunches ("part of the business"); the after-work drink; the predinner cocktail(s) waiting at home; pubs that offer you free snacks with your drink; conventions where free liquor flows day and night; and the exotic and sexy advertising on billboards, on television and in magazines.

Dr. Morris Chafetz, former director of NIAAA, found the "in" and chic aspects of the drinking way of life sinister enough to observe, "There are homes where they don't even say anything to you when you come in the door before they ask, 'What will you have to drink?' In our crazy-quilt value system, masculinity means that if you can hold a lot of alcohol and seemingly not show its effects, that's somehow a sign of strength."

Alcoholics who have achieved sobriety are not reformers

or prohibitionists. They do not oppose drinking, except for themselves. I think social drinking is great—and I wish I could enjoy it—but as I write this I am looking at an advertisement which appeared in Chicago's newspapers. In bold print it proclaims:

"Are you man enough to drink our two-fisted liquor? Our liquor is so rugged and unrelenting, even brutal, to the taste that during the last forty years in Chicago we found only one out of forty-nine men, rarely women, will drink [name of brand] after the first 'shock-glass.' The first is hard to swallow! PERSEVERE! Make it past two 'shock-glasses' and with the third, you could be ours . . . forever."

I think of that first drink when I was nineteen, and that word "forever" sends a shudder down my spine.

EIGHT

The night I walked into the wrong house and nearly scared a sleeping couple out of their wits was probably the night I began realizing I wasn't handling liquor as well as I thought.

It had been a spirited day—a 10 A.M. interview with an actress who liked bloody marys; a multimartini lunch with the news director of a television station; a 4 P.M. cocktail party (there were usually three of these a week); a 5 P.M. interview-on-the-rocks with the producer of a new television series in town to plug the show; and, finally, a dinner show staged by the Chicago Emmy Awards people during which the elbow-bending was strenuous.

I missed the 11:45 P.M. train and the next one was at 1:15 A.M. There was plenty of time to kill and I was primed just enough to want to sustain the glow. A bar located around the corner from the station was still open. Curiously, I was not drunk but something more than mellow when I got off the train in Hinsdale and drove home. I pulled into the driveway, walked through the back door—which was never locked until I got home—hung my coat in the front clothes closet and walked down the hall and into the bedroom. A light went on and I found myself face to face with my astonished neighbors, who were sitting up in bed.

There was little to say or do except go into an "oops—sorry" routine and make a fast exit. I recall that the height of my trauma was not the bedroom confrontation but when I had to return to my car, back out of the driveway and roll a few yards into my own.

In a way, it was an understandable blunder. Our typically suburban houses were look-alikes; their front clothes closet was in the same location as ours, as was their master bedroom, located at the end of a hallway, just like ours. I owned two cars, so I mistook the car in my neighbors' driveway for my other one. For some reason their back door was also unlocked that night.

And I was the sensible drinking man who had never lost his dignity—yet.

Another uncommon incident occurred about a week later, when I was due to speak at the evening affair of a women's club in Wisconsin. I arrived a little early because of heavy snow warnings and drove to the home of the club's chairwoman, as instructed. A small cocktail party was in progress, during which I was to meet the other club officers and a few of her friends.

I always liked a drink before giving a talk, so naturally I had one. This time, however, I had several for no reason except stupidity. Dinner was to follow, so I felt safe. Dinner, however, was an Italian spaghetti affair with wine flowing freely. I don't happen to be especially fond of spaghetti, so I turned my attention to the wine. We drove to the auditorium at the appointed time and the evening appeared to have gone well. Meanwhile, the storm had turned into a miniblizzard and I decided to stay overnight at a motel.

Next morning, in the first fuzzy moments of wakefulness, a horrible realization hit me. I could remember everything of the night before to about midway in my talk;

after that—nothing. I could remember the dinner and the wine and Madame Chairwoman introducing me, and my opening remarks, and a few funny stories to get the audience in the mood, and some serious stuff, and then a total blackout.

I drove home worried, not daring to call my hostess for fear of what I might hear. For a week after that I lived in genuine dread. Had I made an ass of myself? Had I been irreverent, or even offensive? Had I staggered to the lectern? Had I perhaps—horrors—conked out onstage? I did not recall checking into the motel, much less finding it. Everything seemed to have gone well, but why couldn't I remember anything beyond a certain point?

That week was the next thing to hell and made me a nervous wreck. Each time the mail arrived I looked for a Wisconsin postmark, half expecting a letter berating me for having ruined the ladies' evening. Whenever the phone rang, I wondered if it might be the boss, having just heard from Wisconsin.

A week after that horrendous night I did receive a letter from Wisconsin. My hands were moist before I had opened the envelope. It was from Madame Chairwoman, thanking me for having done a great job and mentioning compliments she had received for a fine program. Later I received two or three other complimentary letters from women who had attended. I was surprised and relieved. I was also grateful to the god reputed to watch over soaks.

And I was the sensible drinking man who had never blacked out—yet.

For the most part, my drinking pattern was different from the majority of tipplers. I did not go into bars much, and when I did it was always with something to read. I could never understand how a man could sit on a stool and drink for an hour or two while staring at the mirror or the

bottles on the shelves. I did about half my drinking at the
numerous affairs to which a columnist is invited. (I once
told friends I could probably be drunk every day and it
wouldn't cost me a nickel.) The other half was done at
home, after the children were in bed, and was supported by
about ten pounds of reading material.

One morning, shortly after the Wisconsin near miss, I
awoke a little squiffed. I had been up until three in the
morning and felt that the usual glass of tomato juice
wouldn't be enough. I decided to have an eye-opener,
which turned into a couple of vodkas and orange juice—
doubles. By the time I got off the commuter train in Chicago, I was in no hurry to get to the office (my hours were
my own), bought a newspaper and sauntered into one of
the train station's three bars. I was there about an hour,
after which I felt fit enough to go to work. Outside the
station, near where the skid-row pavement starts, a vagrant
accosted me as I looked for a taxi. He had bloodshot eyes
and dirty clothes, gave off an odor of whisky and vomit,
and looked as if he had slept in a doorway that night. All
he wanted was change for a drink.

Once in the cab, I put a few drops of Murine into my
eyes and a couple of mints into my mouth. I thought of
the plight of the poor devil I had left on the street. How
could a man let himself go to waste like that? How could
he abuse his body and mind and live in degradation? Then
it hit me like a thwack in the ribs:

My God, I'm in worse shape than he is . . .

I looked on him as a shiftless moocher with a filthy coat,
three-day whiskers and a monumental hangover. A lowlife.
A derelict. I saw myself as a regular citizen, bathed and
shaved, with a nice suit, shirt and tie, doing what all decent
men must do to feed their kids and keep them in college. I
was respectable; he was a bum. A parallel came to mind; I

tried to shrug it off but it persisted. And I winced when I reflected that the good-for-nothing out there and I were really fellow travelers; the difference was that he had reached his destination before I had.

And I was the sensible drinking man who never needed a morning snort—until this morning.

I think it was the force of that incident, or the impact of all three in a brief span, that made me realize I could not handle the problem alone. Maybe those people at AA were onto something after all. They certainly had something I didn't have: sobriety.

But a lingering doubt still remained because I had some things they did not have. I had a good position and had never been fired. Yet . . .

I had never been stopped for drunk driving. Yet . . .

I had never had a car accident. Yet . . .

I had never been arrested. Yet . . .

I had never been in a brawl or passed out at a party. Yet . . .

I never had hangovers or missed a column. Yet . . .

I was not a staggering, falling-down drunk. Yet . . .

I had never struck my wife. Yet . . .

Years later I was to become more honest with myself and admit that, true, I had never missed a column, but occasionally I would write two or three in advance so I could safely take a few days off. True, I never had hangovers, but I didn't have to get up at six or seven in the morning. I had all day to write the column and usually took the 10:30 A.M. train, giving me plenty of time to recuperate. True, I had never been in a car accident, but I disliked driving and did as little as necessary because of my fear of putting the quart before the hearse. (I have never opened a bottle in the car lest I might be involved, even innocently, in an accident and the broken seal be used as evidence to destroy me.) True, I had never struck my wife, but I had broken her heart. True, I had never been in jail, but I had slowly built a wall around myself, cutting off first my friends, then my family, then the world and finally God.

And it was true that I was not a staggering, fallen-down drunk. I was a sipper. But I sipped a great deal.

I still found it hard to believe, after becoming a regular in AA, that I was among the unfortunates who were power-less over alcohol. To me a drinking problem was just an-other crisis, and I had had many crises: losing our first home in the Red River valley flood of 1950 and moving to the United States and not knowing a soul in my new coun-try, to name just two. And I had conquered them, or gone around, under or over them, but I had survived. Why shouldn't I be able to handle this crisis? After all, I had willpower.

Some time later Dr. Anderson was to make me think about the latter. "If alcoholism is a disease," he observed, "and I believe it is, what does willpower have to do with it? A cardiac victim can't say, 'I will not have another heart at-tack,' and will it so; the cancer patient can't say, 'I have willpower and I will rid myself of it, I won't let it get worse.' There is something about alcoholism that is organic —physical and psychological in the mind—and willpower doesn't matter. When the alcoholic, after much suffering, vows he'll never take another drink, he really means it at the time. When he winds up drunk a month later, he won-ders what happened; he doesn't realize that willpower has nothing to do with it."

Because I am curious, and because I have spent my life seeking answers to questions, the problem was one messy jumble of doubt and confusion. The famous Rand report is a good example. The report was funded by the National Institute on Alcohol Abuse and Alcoholism, which commissioned the Rand Corporation to study the results of treatment. The report created a huge controversy when it claimed that some recovered alcoholics could safely indulge in moderate drinking. It was criticized by many experts in alcohology, including AA, as giving recovered alcoholics the green light to try social drinking again. Those who believe total abstinence is the safest treatment feared that some alcoholics would die as a result of the report.

But Dr. Morris Chafetz, who commissioned the report when he was director of NIAAA, welcomed its findings and said it might loosen some of the "rigid, stereotypic thinking about treating alcoholism." He argued that the Rand report did not advocate that alcoholics should drink; rather, it had found that patients who took some alcohol and those who did not had similar relapse rates.

"And all they said then," Dr. Chafetz continued, "was, 'Hey, maybe this opens up some new avenues of research about how we are dealing with alcoholic people.' The only reason it was so highly publicized is because people in the treatment field attacked it. They were stating hysterically that there will be two hundred thousand people dying as a consequence of the Rand report.

"I wonder whether that was almost a wish—that they'd sooner have two hundred thousand people die so they could prove their point rather than recognizing that there is not a single study that I know of confirming that an alcoholic person will go down the tubes if he takes a drink.

"I believe many alcoholics do relapse when they take a drink because it is expected of them. Alcoholism experts don't realize that if they keep preaching to these people that they will be lost if they take a drink, well, of course, they'll go down the tubes. And this all-or-nothing philosophy does one other thing. It deters people from seeking help early, when they suddenly notice there's something wrong about their use of alcohol. They think, 'Oh, my God, I've got to make a commitment to stay dry for the rest of my life in a drinking society.' That's pretty tough. So they have to be almost destroyed before they can receive help."

This from the former head of a federal agency. It added to my uncertainty.

One of the first things the doubting drinker is asked to do, if he wants to know whether he is an alcoholic, is to answer a series of questions. One of the best is the series developed by the National Council on Alcoholism. Readers in doubt should try to respond with a simple, honest "yes" or "no" to the following questions, and then place themselves in one of three categories that follow:

1. Do you occasionally drink heavily after a disappointment, a quarrel, or when the boss gives you a hard time?

2. When you have trouble or feel under pressure, do you always drink more heavily than usual?

3. Have you noticed that you are able to handle more liquor than you did when you were first drinking?

4. Did you ever wake up on the "morning after" and discover that you could not remember part of the evening before, even though your friends tell you that you did not pass out?

5. When drinking with other people, do you try to have a few extra drinks when others will not know it?

6. Are there certain occasions when you feel uncomfortable if alcohol is not available?

7. Have you recently noticed that when you begin drinking you are in more of a hurry to get the first drink than you used to be?

8. Do you sometimes feel a little guilty about your drinking?

9. Are you secretly irritated when your family or friends discuss your drinking?

10. Have you recently noticed an increase in the frequency of your memory blackouts?

11. Do you often find that you wish to continue drinking after your friends say they have had enough?

12. Do you usually have a reason for the occasions when you drink heavily?

13. When you are sober, do you often regret things you have done or said while you were drinking?

14. Have you tried switching brands or following different plans for controlling your drinking?

15. Have you often failed to keep the promises you have made to yourself about controlling or cutting down on your drinking?

16. Have you ever tried to control your drinking by making a change in jobs or moving to a new location?

17. Do you try to avoid family or close friends while you are drinking?

18. Are you having an increasing number of financial and work problems?

19. Do more people seem to be treating you unfairly without good reason?

20. Do you eat very little or irregularly when you are drinking?

21. Do you sometimes have the "shakes" in the morning and find that it helps to have a little drink?

22. Have you recently noticed that you cannot drink as much as you once did?

23. Do you sometimes stay drunk for several days at a time?

24. Do you sometimes feel very depressed and wonder whether life is worth living?

25. Sometimes, after periods of drinking, do you see or hear things that are not there?

26. Do you get terribly frightened after you have been drinking heavily?

If you answered "yes" to *any* of these questions, you have some symptoms that may indicate alcoholism. "Yes" answers to three or more questions in various categories indicate the following stages of alcoholism:

Questions 1 to 8: early stage

Questions 9 to 21: middle stage

Questions 22 to 26: beginning of final stage

Surprised? I was. And mortified. The test has a sobering effect on whoever takes it.

But a sobering effect and sobriety, I learned, are two entirely different things.

NINE

A rabbit almost got me to stop drinking.

It happened after I'd been a member of AA for about a year. I was what I would call a periodic regular, in that I would attend meetings regularly for weeks or months and then drop out for a week or two to try "social" drinking. I was *on* the program, not *in* it in a participatory sense, and social drinking never worked. But after a relapse I always returned to the AA fold. Where else could I turn?

I had reached the point of concealing my liquor at home. I had heard so many stories about clever hiding places, I felt my hide-the-hooch system was a work of genius. I was married at the time, and my wife, not knowing the nature of the illness, felt rejected. Thus, when I wanted to sneak a bottle into the house I would tell her that my typewriter needed repair. It was a portable and I would nestle the jug on the keys, clamp down the lid and cloak my treasure from the world. Once home, I would go to the backyard and transfer the juice from the typewriter to the garbage can (about a third of the way down). I got the garbage can idea from another alcoholic who told me he had convinced his wife there were rats around the cans, so she never went near them.

As cunning as this seemed, it had drawbacks. I could only bring the booze into the house when there was nobody inside—and when you have eight children that's a neat trick. Consequently, I was often forced to rummage through the refuse and down quick drinks right there by the garbage. This was not only beneath my dignity, but taking vodka straight from the bottle was not my idea of fun. There was also the risk of forgetting to remove the bottle before the disposal truck came by; many a sad morning I watched my precious hoard being pulverized in the crusher. Further, how long could I continue making up reasons for taking my typewriter out for repair? I gave that gimmick so much mileage, my wife would sometimes say, "That thing's always breaking down. Why don't you get a new one?" My rejoinder was always the same. "You wouldn't understand. A writer gets attached to his typewriter. It's a sentimental thing and I can't part with it."

The night one of the children caught me furtively returning a bottle back to the garbage was when I decided to build a rabbit hutch. We had a couple of fenced-in rabbits (Fibber and Molly) that had dutifully multiplied, so now we had eleven rabbits. The younger children felt it was time they, and the rabbits that would follow, had a decent home, and asked if I would build one. Having such prolific creatures in a household of eight kids was somewhat like carrying coals to Newcastle, and I was less than pleased with the idea. But the youngsters, who had been reading the papers, adopted tactics that were hard to overcome. They engaged in sit-ins, lay-ins, pray-ins, cry-ins and similar demonstrations. They left petitions in what I laughingly called my study (the room that houses the laundry hamper, ironing board, record player, vacuum cleaner and other household items). When they assumed a prone position at the bathroom intersection, thereby halting all important traffic, I capitulated.

I did so with pleasure because it occurred to me that a

hutch, with all the straw and those little beasts bounding about, would be the ideal cache for my flacons. But my talent with hammer and saw was woeful, and when I got through demolishing two orange crates, I couldn't have given away the mess as toothpicks. I called a carpenter.

A rabbit hutch, I discovered, is like nothing else in the world. You must allow for southern exposure and erect a thick side to fend off the north winds and build a screen floor and talc the openings and slant the roof against the rain and install a pull-out tray because rabbits are noted defecators.

As I watched the warren going up on small stilts (the better to dispose óf their void), it seemed to have everything except a garage and air conditioning. Unable to bear the mounting costs, I left to spend more money. There was food to buy—you don't feed carrots to rabbits, except as an occasional treat, because if they get hooked on carrots they'll reject the ordinary fare. They needed "pellets," the complete food. And heavy bowls that wouldn't tip over when they played tag. (I had the impression they played tag all day and far into the night.) And straw. And shavings for the tray. And salt disks for hot weather, and so on. The whole thing, including $12 an hour for the carpenter, cost around $115, but my alcoholic thinking told me it would be well worth it. Wow! My own bar, with a key and furry friends to keep the stuff warm on cold nights. And no more garbage. When thirsty, I could say I was going out to look at the rabbits and meditate, much like others stare at fishbowls.

It was fine for a while, but one night a strange thing happened. As I was reaching into the hutch for my hootch, one of the rabbits—Fibber, Jr., as we called him—hopped up and tried to bite my finger. I didn't know that rabbits bit people, but he was a peculiar one. I'd watched him

playing tag in the daytime, and he clearly had a problem;
he kept trying to mount both males and females. Bad
enough that the rabbits were incestuous, but to have one
that's bisexual and a people-hater was revolting. From then
on, each time I'd reach into the straw that hermaphroditic
hare, nose aquiver, would pounce, leaving ugly scratches on
my wrist. I never knew why Fibber, Jr., had taken a dislike
to me, but after a time the battle for the bottle became too
much of a hazard—spoiled my drinking is what it did—and
I gave him away to a farmer.

At AA meetings, at least, nobody tried to grab my hand,
though there were times when I wished somebody would,
because some nights there were as many, sometimes more,
women than men in attendance. This came as a surprise
because, like many others, I did not associate women with
hard drinking. In my youth, probably because of my Jesuit
schooling, the sentiment was that if a woman smoked in
public she risked being thought of as dissipated, if not
worse. I was to learn that alcoholism is no longer a "man's
disease." A 1958 Gallup survey reported that 55 percent of
American females drank; recent studies indicate the figure
is nearing 75 percent. In at least one Chicago hospital
more than 60 percent of the alcoholics treated in its rehab
unit are women. Alcoholism darbs now say that about half
of the nation's millions of alcoholics are women. Because
of the reluctance of families and physicians to face up to
the problem, however, and because many female alcoholics
are not visible—"pantry drinkers" secure in the safety of
home—the ratio could be higher. In fact, former HEW
Secretary Joseph Califano, Jr., asked Congress in 1979 to
approve additional spending—twenty-two million dollars—
so his department could triple its funds devoted to studying the drinking problems of women.

"It is time to prove to the American people that alcohol-

ism is not only a treatable disease, but a beatable disease,"
he said, emphasizing the "tragic offshoot of alcohol abuse,
fetal alcohol syndrome, the third leading cause of birth defects."

More shocking is the fact that seven out of ten female
alcoholics are also "pill poppers"—addicted to other drugs,
notably Valium and Librium (as told me by Dr. Nelson J.
Bradley, former medical director of the Alcoholic Rehabilitation Center, Lutheran General Hospital, Park Ridge, Illinois).

Muriel Nellis, a member of the Women's Task Panel of
the President's Commission on Mental Health, directed a
year-long HEW study on the problem, which warned that
women are twice as vulnerable as men to alcohol and drug
abuse: "In 1975," she said in a 1978 interview with People
Magazine, "a study showed that 229 million prescriptions
were made out for mood-altering drugs—amphetamines,
sedatives, tranquilizers. That year 80 percent of all prescriptions for amphetamines went to women. More than
two thirds of all the others also went to women.

"It's the increasing stress on women's lives—a husband's
career, the children's needs, the absence of purpose. Also,
the hard sell from the drug industry for quick panaceas is
primarily targeted at women. Pills are more of a way of life
for them. Some doctors have made a great deal of money
providing these quick panaceas. Some simply don't know
that what they are doing is extremely dangerous, but at this
juncture ignorance of the problem should no longer be an
excuse."

I asked Dr. Bradley, who once headed one of the largest
alcoholism rehab units in the Midwest, why so many drinking women also took pills. "I'm ashamed to have to tell
you this," he said, "but it's our fault. It's the fault of the
doctors. Women come to them with depression, change of

life, domestic problems and the like, and doctors take the easy way out. They write prescriptions."

I have met many female alcoholics, and a good number of them boasted that they never had any trouble getting their doctors to prescribe sedatives. One woman told me that in her suburb alone she had three, sometimes four, doctors "on the string" who supplied her with prescriptions whenever she asked. Another said she did not even have to visit her doctor. "I'd make a call and the doctor would make a call and the pills would be at my house in an hour. That was handy when I was hung over."

According to Dr. Roy W. Menninger, president of the Menninger Foundation, "It's a vicious circle. Patients say that they aren't adequately warned by doctors about the hazard of becoming dependent. Doctors say that patients demand these drugs."

The scenario is familiar: Harry is drunk at the dinner party again, spills soup on the hostess and eventually has to be driven home. Friends cluck sympathetically, "Old Harry's smashed again. What a character." But change the roles—Mary gulps too many, has a crying jag and must be helped to the bathroom—and the typical reaction, "Disgusting! How can a woman behave like that?" is sure to follow.

The key word is "disgusting," which is seldom applied to male alcoholics. But the woman has tradition against her; she is the person behind the man, the object of worship placed on a pedestal, the hand that rocks the cradle as she awaits her knight engaged in battle. She is sweetness and desire, and her sacred destiny is motherhood. So how can she degrade herself by drinking? It's senseless!

What doesn't make sense is that Mary and her millions of drinking sisters are branded by the stigma that says they must not become sick, as men do. Society, which doesn't

frown on women who develop diabetes or cancer, is not as
tolerant if they develop alcoholism. Censure exists because
woman, supposedly a creature of endless charm and dignity, must live up to the ideal of "lady." With this double
standard, the drunken man is often considered amusing,
while a woman in the same condition is scorned—an
outcast whose moral flaw should be overcome by "willpower." Hence, the woman afflicted with this disease
comes to doubt her own femininity and turns to alcohol to
shore up her feelings of inadequacy.

Among other things, society decrees that women must
derive a sense of self-worth from their relationship with
men rather than a sense of achievement. The working
woman, for example, is usually identified as working
woman and mother, but who ever heard of working man
and father? The fact is, a woman has three, sometimes
four, roles: mate, homemaker, mother and often working
woman. Society usually gives a man one label, namely, pro-
vider; he is just incidentally lifelong companion and father.

Although many more alcoholic women are "liberating"
themselves to the point of joining AA, many husbands prefer they not join. The husband is embarrassed and
ashamed, afraid that knowledge of his wife's alcoholism
will ruin his career. He may feel she is a business liability,
dragging him down and lessening his chances for success,
so he hides her from his friends and associates. But this
only worsens her feelings of guilt and self-hatred. Subcon-
sciously the husband may like the feeling of mastery which
his wife's helplessness gives him. He runs the show at
home, including being the parent his children turn to for
advice and love. This type of spouse assumes the roles of
controller and martyr; he is the one who visits the children's teacher and attends PTA meetings because his
drinking wife won't leave the house. If the ugly secret is

out, he finds, after a time, that the role of martyr is pleasant. At work his colleagues show sympathy and understanding because when he goes home to dinner, poor fellow, his wife is dead drunk in the bedroom.

This situation also works in reverse: The wife of the alcoholic also gets sympathy from relatives and friends, who praise her for being "both mother and father" to the children. But this often backfires when the husband regains sobriety and control. She wonders why for years she has been unable to get him to stop drinking, yet he ups and joins "a bunch of other drunks" in AA and suddenly he's off the sauce. In some cases the female "martyr" has been known to become jealous of AA and, in a few instances, actually resents his sobriety because she is no longer in control and the object of compassion.

Even when the husband protects and shields his drinking wife out of love, rather than for business or social reasons, he is harming her because this may encourage her to continue drinking. But when the situation can no longer be concealed, when he can no longer tolerate it, when he has had enough, he will generally leave her. A female counselor, herself a recovered alcoholic, told me:

"Most husbands will leave an alcoholic wife. Yet the great majority of nonalcoholic wives will stick it out with drinking husbands, probably because society dictates that a woman must remain by her husband's side come what may, but who can blame the poor man for leaving a lush?

"Because the alcoholic woman is burdened with more guilt and remorse, and is surrounded by secrecy and protection, she has a deeper feeling of being an outcast. So surrender and the decision to take treatment are more difficult. And there are other factors peculiar to the alcoholic woman: After the children are grown, she no longer feels needed. The change of life becomes another emotional hazard, and if she goes out into the working world, she may feel that since she is thinking and working like a man, she must drink like a man.

"It's important for the alcoholic woman to find her own identity, not as something corelated to male identity but to her own meaningful life. It's a fact of life that in the working world she's likely to be a loser, through lack of opportunity, and may not know how to compete.

"Luckily, society's attitudes are getting more liberal and women alcoholics are coming out of hiding more and seeking treatment at an earlier stage of the disease. So one liberalizing force that tends to increase the number of women alcoholics—the acceptance of women into business and professional fields and into today's drinking culture—also gives us more hope for their recovery. But it's got to be faced that more women will become alcoholic in the future because more women will be drinking, and more women will also be feeling the pressures of the real world as they go out, unprotected now.

"But once they're taken off the pedestal and seen as real people, with defects as well as virtues, women will no longer have to feel guilty about falling from grace if they develop alcoholism, and will accept it as the disease it is. It's at this point that the road to treatment starts."

But women, spunky as they are, cannot do it alone. They need more help and consideration in the area of treatment. For example, there are more than seven thousand public and private treatment facilities in this country, but only forty are exclusively for women. Muriel Nellis complains that the majority of alcoholism and drug treatment programs are male-oriented, and women are reluctant to seek help in sexually integrated settings. "It's a fact," she says, "that many male alcohol and drug addicts show contempt for their female counterparts, so coeducational therapy has not been effective."

The help women need is urgent, because the female drinker has a tougher time of it all along the line. She hits the skids faster; it takes eight to ten years for the female alcoholic to reach the chronic stage of alcoholism, compared to ten to fifteen years for the male. The woman's liver becomes damaged more rapidly than that of the man, and there is a definite relation between heavy drinking and obstetric and gynecologic problems. In the area of stress, she is more vulnerable because of childbearing and menopause, more prone to pills and, for hormonal reasons, gets drunk faster than men who consume equivalent amounts of alcohol.

The fact that smaller quantities of alcohol are consumed by most women does not necessarily mean that they are genteel sippers. One middle-aged recovered female alcoholic told me, "What woman would go a day or two without combing her hair? I did when I was drinking. I tell you the God's truth, that before I came to my senses I went four months without once putting a comb or a brush to my hair. Not four days. Four months! That's what I call drinking."

During one of my hospital stays, I met the son of a seventy-year-old woman who had come to treatment for the first time in a long life of drinking. He confided that the last time he had been to her home—she lived alone—he had found an incredible 163 empty half-pints in her bedroom. One day, when she was in a jovial mood, I teased her about it.

"I've heard of people hiding a bottle or two under the mattress," I said, "but where could you possibly put 163?"

"One hundred and sixty-four!" she snapped.

TEN

Alcoholism has been described as "cunning, baffling and powerful," and when I think of cunning I think of Leonard.

Leonard was a man of many talents and faces—drunkard, priest, professional golfer, recovered alcoholic and, finally, alcoholism counselor. The vocations were for real, except those of priest and golf pro; in those areas he was a calculated phony, but he fooled a lot of people for a time.

He had many things going for him. He had a brilliant business career until he abandoned himself to the bottle and became a full-time drunk. A lean man in his early fifties, he had a rollicking personality, with a laugh to match, and more nerve than a sky diver. He was also a consummate actor, a gift that served him well, because he did not like to spend money.

Leonard was not the type to sidle up to strangers in bars and cadge drinks. This was beneath him, because he always went first class. Aware that most people are impressed by celebrity status, he would assume the roles of priest or golfer coming to or from a tournament, depending on his mood or what town he was in. He frequented only the elegant, high-toned lounges, and his usual stunt was to engage the bartender in conversation and casually mention he was

Father so-and-so, on vacation and was expecting a telephone call. Then he would retire to a nearby table and sip
in silence.

"Just telling the tapster I was a priest," he said, "was
usually good for a drink on the house. After a while word
would get around that the nice-looking fellow over there by
himself was a priest, and sooner or later somebody would
drift by and offer to buy me a drink. Some of these guys really wanted to talk; they had something on their minds,
usually a woman problem.

"Oh, the advice I used to give! You see, their conscience
bothered them and it made them feel good to get cozy
with a priest. They'd tell me about their wives and girl
friends, and what did I think of separation, and could they
keep their church standing if they got divorced, and so on.
One night a guy went all the way. He wasn't drunk, but
he'd had enough to tell me he hadn't been to confession
for years, and would I hear his confession then and there?
Of course I told him it was hardly the place for confession,
but I made him promise he'd go to church next Sunday."

Leonard told me he always wore a black suit for these
excursions and sometimes felt cocky enough, "when business was bad," to wear a Roman collar in the shebeen.

"But I had no trouble attracting people. They liked to
come to the table and say, 'Let me buy you a drink, Father.' Any night I could always count on the character
who'd say, 'I'm not Catholic, Father, but I'd be honored to
buy you a drink.' I think some of them used me, too. I vis-
ualized them going home, tanked, and telling their wives,
'Honey, I ran into this priest and we got into a long discussion on birth control and I just couldn't pull away.' The
point is that in the three or four days I'd spend in that
hotel, I'd spend damn little of my own money on booze.

And there was often what I call the big fringe benefit: I'd get invited home for the night or weekend by some of these people, especially when I'd complain that my room was too warm or too cold. They got a thrill out of doing that. I have a big capacity for liquor, but I hold it well and, as a priest, I'd be on my good behavior. Once I stayed nine days at the estate of some millionaire who insisted I be his guest. He had a swimming pool and servants—glorious vacation."

At other times Leonard posed as a golfer on the tournament circuit. He was an ordinary player, but he had a thorough knowledge of professional tournaments, the players and their performance. He'd saunter to the bar with his spiffy clubs and, invariably, the barkeep would ask about his game.

"I'd tell him I was in town for a tournament that was starting that week, or back from one that just ended somewhere. I'd give him a fake name and explain I wasn't one of the big stars, but I usually came in in the fair-to-low money. Now you know that most people, even those who read the sports pages, don't recognize the names of golfers who wind up in fourteenth or twentieth place. So I was the not-too-successful but steady pro, and that would get me my first drink from the bartender, and I'd head for a quiet table. You'd be amazed at how much people are fascinated by golf pros. There were the golf nuts themselves, hero-worshipers, who liked the idea of drinking with a pro. And there were the guys who didn't play golf but insisted on buying me drinks because of what they would tell their friends at the office next day. I follow the game pretty good, so I could pull it off when they asked me for pointers, or what Ben Hogan was really like."

But Leonard met his match one night. "I was a priest," he recounted, "and I was sitting with an engaging fellow.

He told me he was a traveling salesman, and as we got more friendly he confided he was an alcoholic who'd just fallen off the wagon. He felt so bad about it, I couldn't keep up the playacting, so finally I leaned over and said, 'Don't feel too bad about it. But I'm going to let you in on a secret. I'm not really a priest.'

"Well, the guy stared at me for half a minute, no expression on his face. Then he leaned over and said, 'I'll let you in on a secret. I am.' Sure enough, he was an alcoholic priest posing as a salesman on a toot. We were both playing roles. How's that for coincidence?"

The first time I ran into an alcoholic priest, I was stunned. This was harder to believe than my first encounter with an alcoholic doctor. After all, who is closer to spirituality, to God, than a priest? I didn't stop to think that a priest is, first, a man with the strengths and frailties of other men. I'm sure the reason it took me so long to understand alcoholism in the clergy is that I was so close to it in my formative years—kindergarten nuns and two Jesuit colleges. I have since met more than a dozen priests who have the ailment. One of them threw some light on the disease in a letter responding to my questions:

"When some people hear the word 'spirituality' they immediately think someone is trying to tell them to go to church. It isn't that at all. In recovery we speak of a higher power, which some people prefer to call God. The recovering alky comes to realize that there's really a power greater than himself that will direct his life if given some cooperation. To be a spiritual person doesn't mean to be a religious person. Spirituality doesn't include formal religion, and it doesn't necessarily exclude the practice of your religion. Spirituality for the alky means the newly found or rediscovered sense of the joy of living.

"For the alky, daily existence is a problem to be endured

rather than a joy. Guilt, fear and resentment are emotions that every normal person tries to avoid in life. The alky tries to avoid them, too—by drinking. The very things the alky tries to avoid are the very things that beome more and more prominent and overpowering. It's only when he realizes that he can't rid himself of these emotions that he looks for help. That help is another person, or group of people, or something else that the alky recognizes as more powerful than himself. When he says okay to whatever his higher power is, a little hope appears. If he sticks with that hope he'll get to believe that there is someone or something that can end his misery.

"Then comes probably the most difficult step: surrendering to that higher power, whatever it is. This is when he finally realizes he can't do it alone. But with the help of his higher power he's also got to get some extra help, like a treatment center, professional counseling, AA or whatever it is that works for him. Everybody would like to be good, and the alky finally figures out that goodness for him is possible only if he surrenders to his higher power. He first comes to hope, then to believe that his higher power is willing to accept him as he is, and also willing to make something better out of him if he'll cooperate. It sounds simple, but I was a suffering alky and I know how tough it was to accept that not only was I not all-powerful, but I was powerless over the influence of one of my higher power's creations—alcohol. Surrender is a simple-sounding word, but it's not an easy move. But spirituality, for the recovering alky, is fairly simple, and that's how I'm making it."

The ratio of alcoholics to nonalcoholics varies among the vocations. The rate among doctors, for example, is 10 percent, which is the rate for the general population. The rate among the clergy could be less, probably because men of the cloth encounter fewer occasions to drink than people in the layman's world. Some alcoholic priests have told me, making a "rough guess," that they believe at least 8 percent of the Catholic clergy suffer from alcoholism. The National Conference of Catholic Bishops, however, places the figure at 5 percent. The report, prepared by the Bishops' Committee on Priestly Life and Ministry, reveals that clergy-related alcoholism is more than a big-city problem: "The data from this survey indicate that it is proportionately present in the smallest as well as the largest dioceses and religious orders. [But] 75 percent of the clergy who have undergone treatment for alcoholism maintain sobriety."

Every Catholic archdiocese has some system to monitor priests with a drinking problem. Typical is the archdiocese of Hartford, Connecticut, whose program for alcoholic priests depends on the cooperation of other priests. The policy of the archbishop's office is to direct priests to be alert to possible alcoholism problems in fellow priests and to refer them to one member of a special panel of eight peers set up by the archdiocese. Members of this group, who are all volunteers, offer counseling and, when necessary, refer the priests to treatment agencies for further help.

Alcoholic priests may also be referred to the archbishop's office, which will, in turn, refer them for help to a member of the special panel. The archbishop's policy statement stresses that the archdiocese recognizes alcoholism as an illness "which demands our enlightened concern." It adds that the program is designed to help alcohol or drug-addicted priests "regain that state of health and well-being which will allow for productive and rewarding ministry."

The program is loosely structured; there is no center or office for the volunteer personnel because the counseling is done on a confidential, one-on-one basis. Existing treatment facilities within the community are often used, but when the need arises patients are sent outside the area to such places as Guest House, in Lake Orion, Michigan, and Affirmative House, in Worcester, Massachusetts, established solely for the treatment of priests addicted to alcohol or other chemicals.

A priest in the archdiocese will not lose his assignment because of alcoholism as long as he seeks help in overcoming the problem; his superiors will go "to any lengths" to provide him with assistance, according to a spokesman. However, if the alcoholism is so severe as to cause possible harm to the parish, the priest is usually relieved of his duties and an effort is made to get him to acknowledge his problem and get further help.

A clue as to how the Catholic Church looks upon the problem comes from one of its leaders, the late Bishop Fulton J. Sheen: "The drunkard is a sinner; the alcoholic has a pathological condition with which there is associated a psychological obsession that he must drink. A drunkard could stop drinking if he wanted to; an alcoholic may not want to get drunk, but he is overwhelmed by an irresistible impulse. The drunkard is what he is because of wrong choices at the present moment; the alcoholic is what he is because of wrong choices in the past."

Father Gerald, another tosspot friend of mine, is less gentle with himself: "I was a lush," he said. "The only difference between me and your typical wino was that I wore a Roman collar and I stayed away from skid row."

Father Gerald, who drank heavily for twenty-eight years, is a Jesuit who now counsels other alcoholic priests. Looking back, he is convinced he was an alcoholic from his very first drink, which consisted of a glass of wine consumed when he was twenty-two:

"I loved the taste of it right away. It was made in our vineyards in California and it gave me a glow. I was a newly arrived seminarian and we were given a glass of wine with dinner. After that first glass I knew I wanted another. Within a week I had figured out who were the nondrinkers and I'd head for their table because I could get their drinks. One day some of us were invited to a party and I had my first mixed drink, a manhattan. I had three of those within thirty-five minutes—already I was gulping— and I had to be taken home. I couldn't walk.

"From the beginning, in the novitiate, I noticed that booze gave me a real lift. In my last year of training there was always this desire for more. After ordination I noticed that I hung around only with priests who drank. Some Saturdays we drank the night through, and I didn't think that was bad. I remember that I never wanted to get drunk, that I seldom had aftereffects, and I was usually the guy who drove the others home. That was the clue that I was an alcoholic—the growing tolerance. I could handle it. I never thought of it then, but that was the warning sign.

"I was lonely, and loneliness is a very strong factor in the alcoholic. In 1961, after eighteen years of drinking, I joined AA, but I really didn't buy it. I'd go to meetings, then run back to my room to drink; I figured my work was more important than going to meetings. I did that for ten more years in AA before I finally quit for good. I could admit that I was an alcoholic at the head level, intellectually, but not at the gut level. I always figured I could control it. Besides, I rationalized I couldn't be an alcoholic because I drank mostly wine. God, how I loved that stuff. For quite a while I was the one who ordered the Mass wine for the rectory, so I had no problems. Church funds paid for it, and my share, too."

At Mass, most priests take about a third or half of the

cruet of wine, which is 18 percent alcohol. But not Father Gerald. He often drained it after a night of drinking, taking the wine on an empty stomach. Then he'd head out to breakfast with a pleasant buzz. The problems got worse as the drinking increased: guilt, fear, blackouts, arriving late for Mass and trying to keep his boozy breath from wafting through the grate in the confessional. Once, after being sober for a few months, he decided that "just one drink" during a fund-raising benefit would be harmless. "I wound up plastered and dancing with every woman in the place," he said, "and I had my collar on. That's a no-no in the church, and I caught hell for it."

On another occasion he fell down a long flight of stairs in a private home and his face slammed into the windowsill at the bottom. He lost his front teeth (and eventually had to get a denture), and although he was bleeding profusely from the mouth and his face was cut up, he insisted on saying Mass next morning. "At this point I was into the morning shakes," he recalled, "and I had this obsessive fear that some time I would drop the Communion Host down some woman's brassiere."

Father Gerald, who has been counseling alcoholic priests in recent years, disagrees with the 5 percent ratio of clergy-related alcoholism estimated by the National Conference of Catholic Bishops. "From my experience, it's more like 12 percent," he said. "The denial syndrome is terribly strong among priests; can you imagine what it must be for a bishop or a cardinal?"

Father Gerald's last drink was just before Christmas 1971, and his feeling that day was not one of remorse and guilt. "It was plain disgust, but it finally got through that there was no way I could do it alone—there has to be intervention for priests—and I'd have to surrender, totally, because I was licked."

Today, when Father Gerald says Mass, there is no wine in the cruet. He enjoys a dispensation handed down by the Vatican in 1974 that permits recovered priests to drink unfermented grape juice instead of wine. I wondered if he ever thought of wine now during Consecration.

"Oh, yes," he said, "always. But I also think of the trouble it got me in. Especially the time I came so close to being thrown out of the seminary. I woke up one morning and the surroundings were strange. I opened the door to see what number was on it; it wasn't mine. I was in the wrong bed in the wrong room. Luckily, the priest in whose bed I passed out was out of town. The rector happened along and saw me coming out of the wrong room. And you know what I told him? I told him I'd been sleepwalking.

"Thank God he bought it, because I don't think I'd be where I am, and what I am, today."

ELEVEN

A thirsty nun pedaling a bicycle to the liquor store? Why not? Other people do it. And nuns are people.

At the beginning, meeting a priest who was an alcoholic was invariably a shock to me. All sorts of questions disturbed my thoughts. How could a man get drunk who communed so much with God? After drinking themselves into a stupor, how could they make it to six o'clock Mass? What if a priest was blotto and was suddenly called upon to take over a wedding or funeral? Worse, what happened to their bodies and minds if they hadn't reached the fermented-grape stage and drank the wine at Consecration? I found it all very bewildering. But the astonishment grew when I discovered that the holy orders also included nuns who were alcoholics. Why, nuns had to travel in pairs when they left the convent and wore habits (in those days) that were conspicuous. I could understand a priest, in sports clothes, entering a liquor store after a golf game. But nuns!

I know several alcoholic nuns, recovered and some of them now dedicated to counseling other alcoholics. One of them told me, "When the alarm went off in the morning, I did two things with one hand motion. I'd shut off the alarm and pick up the half-filled tumbler of straight vodka next to it. I had to polish that off before I could even get up and brush my teeth. And, of course, like everybody else I thought that vodka had no smell.

"Getting the liquor wasn't much of a problem. I have a lot of relatives and friends, and on birthdays and church holidays and special occasions they always gave me gifts— expensive prayer beads and books and statuettes and things like that. So I'd tell them, 'Next Tuesday we're celebrating the feast of Saint so-and-so at the convent, and I think the sisters would appreciate a little spirits for the occasion.' And they'd say, 'Fine, Sister, I'll bring over a few bottles of wine.' And I'd say, 'Oh, we have wine at the convent, you know, for Easter and Christmas, and for medicine. But don't you think the sisters might enjoy a change? I think brandy or vodka would be nice—just a little something different.'

"If you look at the church calendar, you'll see that we honor some saint on just about every day of the year. So, you see, I had no problem coming up with special occasions for a 'sacred toast,' as I called it.

"There was something else. Some of these donors, while they didn't suspect I had a problem, sort of knew that I liked a nip now and then, and when they'd bring it over they'd slip me an extra bottle ('This one's for you, Sister'). I guess they thought that was sort of cute. Because I was able to get so many of these gifts, I was pretty well in charge of the liquor that came in, and Mother Superior never knew that I kept most of it in my room. When I knew I had to be out of my room for a while—I taught fourth grade—I would pour booze in medicine bottles and tape them around my legs so I wouldn't be without it, no matter where I had to be. Nobody ever sees a nun's legs."

I wondered if the gurgle of the bottles as she strode down the corridors ever gave her away. "Remember," she said, "I had a long string of beads hanging from my waist, and a heavy ring of keys, and the jinglejangle of those beads and keys drowned out the gurgle around my legs."

I asked the nun if her drinking ever got her into trouble. "Not much," she said. "I just sipped during the day and the serious drinking came only after we retired to our rooms for the night. So I was pretty safe. I had a close call one night when I was taking a shower. This was real dumb, but I took a bottle of scotch with me to the shower. You can imagine what happened with all that soap on my hands; the bottle slipped out and broke into a hundred pieces on the floor. How do you get rid of a smell like that in a steamy shower room? No one else saw it happen, but I almost panicked. I was too tight to pick up all that broken glass. One of the nuns was a very dear friend and I decided to spill the beans and ask her to help me. I'll never forget what she said when she came back with me to the showers: 'Mother of God, it smells like a brewery!' It was winter and we opened all the windows that worked and left them open all night, and we picked up every bit of glass, but I tell you, I prayed extra hard that night. It turned out later, when I was released from my vows, that my friend and a couple of other nuns knew what I was up to. But this was something they didn't understand, so nobody did anything about it. That's the tragedy—you can't hide drinking like mine when you're living the communal life, but nobody, in those days, knew what to do about it."

Another nun told me there were some advantages for the alcoholic in communal living. "When you spend your days and nights in a convent and school," she said, "you find a hundred places to hide liquor. For two years I kept a pint on the top of the bookshelf right in the classroom, behind my books, the ones the children never touched. After class was out, I'd have a couple of good long swallows before going back to the convent. Another good place was in the basement, where we kept boxes of candles. There was always a carton in that stack that didn't have candles. It had my supply."

This nun said that one autumn night, after dusk, she discovered that her supply had run out. She excused herself when the community was in chapel for evening vespers, moved a ladder to the second-floor window of her room, and parked a bicycle next to the ladder. "Kids were always leaving their bikes around the yard," she recalled. "That was no problem, but to this day I don't know how I got that ladder up there. It just shows you what a desperate alcoholic will do."

Later, when the nuns were in their rooms for the night, she changed into slacks and a sweater she kept in her closet, clambered down the ladder, mounted the bicycle and pedaled furtively to a liquor store two blocks away.

"You make it sound so easy," I said.

"It wasn't that bad," the nun said. "I was lucky. The bike had a basket on the handlebars. But I didn't know that at the time, and I sometimes think of that night. What if the bike had no basket? How would I have brought that bottle back? I don't know how to ride a bicycle one-handed."

The nun went on to say that her most embarrassing experience was when she was carrying four cans of beer from the basement to her room. "I had them tucked inside my habit, below the bosom, and you couldn't tell I had a load in there. Then I ran into Mother Superior near the staircase. We were making small talk, when one of the cans slipped out of place and dropped to the floor with a big thud, right at her feet!"

"How did you explain it?"

"What was there to explain? I was caught dead to rights. Fortunately, Mother Superior knew I was leaving the order; we had talked about it before. I knew that the holy orders were not for me—I hadn't taken the final vows—and she knew that I had some kind of problem with drink. But she didn't know how to handle it. I know she would have wanted to do something, but she had no idea it was that serious, and I think she thought it would just go away somehow. I think the whole thing frightened her because she didn't understand. Anyway, I apologized, picked up the can and said, 'Well, Mother, soon you won't have me around to give you all this trouble.' She was very nice about it, but I knew she was hurt. I saw her eyes glisten when I turned away. And that night, in my room, there were tears in my eyes, too."

These incidents made me realize (since I denied that I could be an alcoholic because of my background) that alcoholism is no respecter of person. It touches everyone—even in convents and in the house of God.

I have dwelled at length here on the Catholic clergy, perhaps because I found it easy to identify with the priests. It is certainly not my intention to suggest that the Catholic orders are singularly prone to the disease. That is not the case; alcoholism strikes everywhere, and the various Protestant and other denominations are no exception, as I see it. It happens that a Catholic priest who is an alcoholic is more of an attention getter than, say, a Methodist minister. A Catholic priest does not have wife-and-children-and-diapers problems, for example. The Baptist cleric does, and when he discusses his drinking problem it is somewhat different from that of the Catholic priest, who lives a life of celibacy and takes vows of chastity, obedience and poverty. I did notice, over the years, an unusual number of Protestant ministers' wives taking treatment. (One of them told me that because her "dull-dull-dull" Lutheran-minister husband was usually home, "some days I practically lived in the laundromat, where he couldn't see me drinking my life away.") And I also found that the claim that Jews never became alcoholics was a myth; I have encountered a fair representation.

But it does appear true that alcoholism is more prevalent among certain nationalities. Dr. Chavetz pointed out that in some countries—he singled out Italy and Israel—drinking is an accepted social custom, but alcoholism is uncommon. The reason, he suggested, was that in those countries alcohol was a happy companion to an occasion, not the occasion itself. Several other countries, notably France and the Soviet Union, have a higher rate of alcoholism than the United States. (France has the highest.) Russian newspapers now attribute more than 60 percent of that nation's major crime to liquor. Even Communist Party chief Leonid Brezhnev publicly acknowledged the problem during a visit from Henry Kissinger when the latter was Secretary of 'State. Discussing plans for an American soft-drink factory in the Soviet Union, he said, "Maybe we can teach our people to drink less vodka and more Pepsi-Cola."

At a 1980 congress on alcoholism held in Warsaw, it was officially made public that drinking is now the number one social problem in Poland, a country that, like other Communist nations, once considered alcoholism a capitalist disease. Poles drink about seven times as much alcohol as they did before World War II, and about one third of their food budget is spent on alcohol. According to the Polish government report, about one million Poles (one in thirty-five) get drunk every day, 90 percent of all assaults are committed by people under the influence, and each year almost nine hundred thousand people require medical treatment for alcohol-related injuries or disorders. The study, conducted by the Polish Ministry of Labor, Wages and Social Affairs, said that one worker out of every thirty-nine is regularly drunk on the job and drink abuse accounts for nine hundred million dollars in losses of the Polish economy every year. A Krakow judge, Mikolaj Tolkan, stunned the congress by saying that if the present rate of drinking continues, the population will drink itself into oblivion by the year 2000.

The program for alcoholic priests in the archdiocese of Hartford resembles a program for alcoholic lawyers started in 1976 by the California Bar Association. In many states, disbarment has been the fate of attorneys whose drinking has led to disciplinary action or criminal activity. But in California, lawyers and judges with a drinking problem are given a chance at rehabilitation with the help of fellow bar members serving as volunteers. The program is run by the bar's Committee on Alcohol Abuse, made up of thirteen judges and lawyers. Assistance is offered not only to lawyers facing disciplinary action but also to others whose problems have been detected at an early stage.

Similar programs are in operation in Minnesota, New Jersey, Arizona, Colorado, North Dakota, New York, Washington, Wisconsin, Connecticut, Massachusetts, South Carolina, Hawaii, North Carolina and Illinois, which joined the fold in 1980.

According to members of the California committee, alcohol abuse is responsible for two thirds of the disciplinary actions taken against California lawyers. About half the lawyers in the bar's rehabilitation program are referred to it as a result of disciplinary hearings. Participation in the program is mandatory for some lawyers as a condition for keeping their license to practice. According to a counselor who serves as a consultant to the California program, "Getting a judge or attorney to admit to having a problem is especially difficult. Lawyers are always giving advice to other people, but they resist taking it themselves. Their alibi structure is strong. They can offer a thousand excuses [as to] why they drink."

Members of the bar who aid fellow lawyers are called panelists. There are about two hundred panelists throughout California. Three panelists from the alcoholic person's area are assigned to each new case. The panelists, all recovered alcoholics, offer support, take the sufferers to AA meetings (if they are inclined to attend) and, where indicated, recommend treatment. One judge on the committee emphasized that panelists are prohibited from "relieving the participant of personal responsibilities; they do not go to court for him, pay his hospital bills or office expenses, or represent him before disciplinary committees."

The panelists claim that the success rate so far is roughly 65 percent. Further, a few lawyers who were disbarred for drinking before the program started have been reinstated after being admitted to the program. The attorneys who go into the program are guaranteed strict confidentiality. The identity of the participants is never revealed to the bar's disciplinary committees. "The only time we report on a person's progress to such an agency," one panelist said, "is where a participant was a disciplinary case to begin with."

In 1974 *Time* magazine's cover story on alcoholism stated, "Some experts believe that alcoholism may be encouraged by the destruction of traditional values. Buttressing this notion is the experience of American Indians and Eskimos, whose cultures have been disrupted more than those of any other ethnic groups on the continent. 'The major problem is one of social disintegration,' says Dr. Charles Hudson, chief of psychiatric services at the U. S. Public Health Service's Alaska Native Medical Center. 'The original social structure in many places in rural Alaska has been blown apart, much as it has been in central cities, the ghettos and Appalachia. The things that were important to people have been taken away and when there's nothing to do, they'll take their last buck to get a bottle and stay drunk all the time.'

"Blacks and Chicanos are also particularly prone to alcoholism, possibly for similar reasons. Among whites, the Irish Americans probably rank highest on the alcoholic scale. No one can explain precisely why, although Irish American social life has often centered around the pub or bar, and heavy drinking has been a culturally accepted means for temporarily getting away from problems. Jews, by contrast, have a relatively low incidence of alcoholism, though it is rising among them too. ('Jews eat when they have problems,' quips one Jewish psychiatrist in Manhattan.)

"Although alcoholism often follows ten years or so of problem drinking, there are also alcoholics who apparently skipped even the social-drinker phase. They passed from total abstinence directly into chronic alcoholism. This may be due to a biochemical imbalance of some sort."

I showed the *Time* article to one of my alcoholic priest friends and said, "See? The French are the world's biggest drinkers, and the Irish are prone to alcoholism. My mother was French and my father was Irish, my great-grandfather was part Indian, and on top of that I think I skipped the social-drinker stage and was an instant alcoholic. I had three strikes against me right from the start."

I did not get any sympathy from him, but I did get what he called his favorite drinking story:

After delivering his very first sermon, the newly ordained priest asked his superior how he had done. "Not bad," said the Monsignor, "but you seemed nervous and a bit scared. Next time, put some vodka in the glass of water in the pulpit. It'll relax you and loosen you up." The following Sunday the young priest did as instructed and talked up a

storm. Again he asked his boss for comment on his performance. "You were more relaxed," the Monsignor said,
"but there are a few mistakes we should straighten out:

"1) There are Ten Commandments, not Twelve; 2)
There are twelve apostles, not ten; 3) You must not, ever
again, describe Jesus Christ as the late J.C.; 4) David simply slew Goliath; he did not kick the hell out of him; and
finally, the Father, the Son and the Holy Ghost are not to
be referred to as Big Daddy, Junior and The Spook."

TWELVE

When my friend, Dr. Mike, told me he had delivered twins when triplets were expected, then hustled off for a cigarette as the third baby was arriving, I was incredulous. But when I read about the New York obstetrician who tried to do a surgical procedure without first inserting a blade in the surgical knife, I became curious—fearful, really—about addiction among doctors. I think my interest was partly meant to assuage my own guilt and self-dislike, especially since I had not given myself to AA with honesty. Also, it was muscled by my admiration for Dr. Anderson, of the Hinsdale San, who, at the other end of the scale, had never imbibed yet was so dedicated to the rehabilitation of victims of the curse.

In 1971 a Silver Spring, Maryland, general practitioner was convicted of assault and battery against a young woman during a house call. Alerted by the woman's complaint against him for a previous incident, Montgomery County police watched over closed-circuit television while the doctor gave her two injections and tried to rape her, according to trial testimony.

In 1975 Cyril and Stewart Marcus, twin obstetricians at New York Hospital–Cornell Medical Center, were found dead as a result of acute barbiturate withdrawal. During the months preceding their deaths, the hospital's nursing staff had reported incidents in which other doctors had to be summoned to complete operations for both brothers because of their shaky hands and unsteady balance. In one of these incidents, Dr. Cyril had tried to perform surgery with a knife that had no blade.

In 1977 a physician at a Washington, D.C., hospital was summoned on two separate occasions to provide emergency care for two elderly women with temperatures higher than 106 degrees. In neither case did he examine the patients adequately or order laboratory tests; he treated one with enemas and the other with vitamins plus enemas. The second woman died eight hours later of a surgically treatable abdominal condition that probably was made worse by the enemas. Because of similar complaints against this physician dating back at least ten years, his professional ability was reviewed by the hospital's credentials committee and he was told that he could no longer practice in the hospital except under direct supervision.

My curiosity about such scandals led me into further research which indicated that unethical behavior and disability stemming from addiction were more serious than the medical profession publicly acknowledged.

In the summer of 1977 Newsweek magazine did a major story on addiction in the medical field which quoted the American Medical Association as admitting that at least one hundred addicted doctors committed suicide every year, a number "equivalent to the size of the average graduating class" of a typical medical school. At about the same time, one of the AMA's publications, Advocate, reported that estimates of psychologically impaired physicians ranged from 5 to 10 percent: "Physicians strongly resist recognition of the fact that they or any of their peers can become ill. A 'cloak of silence' has been the usual reaction. But the need to protect the public and preserve the integrity of the medical profession has made this course untenable." In November 1974 the AMA drafted the Disabled Physicians Act, which recommended that state medical associations be given authority to act as agents of the licensing boards in examining doctors alleged to be sick and in evaluating their ability to practice. Thirty-one states have enacted legislation related to professionally impaired physicians.

Dr. Herbert Modlin of the Menninger Foundation in Topeka, Kansas, developed a profile of the sick doctor based on a study of thirty such patients. Almost all had unsatisfactory marriages and practiced alone, depriving themselves of psychological support. Most had had neurotic problems since childhood and had turned to alcohol and/or drugs in the age range of thirty-five to forty-five. Typically, they had denied having a problem to everyone, including themselves. Most doctors had started on barbiturates because they couldn't sleep, then had taken amphetamines to overcome morning drowsiness. One patient, a San Francisco surgeon, got into trouble after his mother died of cancer and his wife left him for another man. He drank at night, took barbiturates during the day and eventually escalated to two or three daily shots of the narcotic Demerol. Every single doctor I know who was addicted was on both alcohol and other mood-altering drugs.

Aside from the daily trauma of work, there are other reasons why doctors turn to alcohol and drugs. The stress of a busy practice lures them to find relief in their own little black bags. "How long can you keep prescribing drugs for tension, anxiety, fatigue and depression before you decide to use them yourself?" asked Dr. G. Douglas Talbott of the Medical Association of Georgia.

Disciplining the errant doctor has always been difficult. Physicians are reluctant to bring accusations against a colleague. They do not wish to become involved in drawn-out disciplinary proceedings, and they fear slander suits. Of the nearly twelve hundred complaints against practitioners brought to the attention of New York State authorities in 1977, only thirty-one came from other doctors. Moreover, the mechanism for taking action has become so cumbersome as to render disciplinary laws somewhat ineffective, although a number of legal roadblocks are gradually being removed.

Dr. Matthew Ross, a professor at the University of California at Irvine and chief psychiatrist at the Long Beach Veterans Administration Hospital, said he wanted doctors to take better care of their sick colleagues. He accused the medical profession of "abandoning" fellow doctors who need help:

"They have self-doubts and suddenly life becomes very threatening, because of depression and addiction," he said. "Doctors tend to neglect their own physical and emotional disabilities and do not ask for help early enough.

"And, worse," Dr. Ross went on, "we neglect these physicians." He urged that other doctors be more "paternalistic" toward their troubled colleagues. According to him, doctors have a suicide rate of 37.7 per 100,000, compared with the average American male rate of 34.6 per 100,000. But among female doctors the suicide rate is four times what it is among other women.

Dr. Ferris N. Pitts, Jr., professor of psychiatry at the University of Southern California School of Medicine in Los Angeles, stated, in May 1979, that women doctors were committing suicide at an alarming rate. He said studies were needed to find out what kind of women went into medicine and what happened to them once they entered practice.

A survey of death notices published in the *Journal of the*

American Medical Association between 1967 and 1972 revealed that one in every fifteen deaths of female physicians was a suicide, according to Dr. Pitts. Drug overdose was the typical form of suicide and the average age of women doctors who took their own lives was forty-seven, as reported by Dr. Pitts in the May 1979 issue of the *American Journal of Psychiatry*.

"The majority of these premature deaths occurred during what should be years of productive professional life," Dr. Pitts said. He added that the suicide rate among women doctors is twice as high as that for divorced women over the age of seventy, the group of women previously thought to have the highest suicide rate. Three quarters of the women who killed themselves were diagnosed as being victims of alcoholism or depression.

The report of Dr. Matthew Ross is even more alarming. It states that more doctors commit suicide than die by drowning, plane and auto accidents. Figures show that up to 22,000 (or almost 7 percent) of the nation's 324,000 medical doctors are or will become alcoholics. Doctors are 30 to 100 times more likely to resort to the use of tranquilizers, sedatives and stimulants than the average person, with most of the drug victims attributing their problem to overwork and fatigue. He said much of the overwork may stem from self-doubts and feelings of inferiority, causing a need to compensate by working harder. "There are no immediate answers," Dr. Ross said, adding that "our knowledge remains incomplete, inconclusive and sporadic."

The AMA was sufficiently concerned about the problem to have held two national conferences in the last decade to discuss it. At one of the conferences, doctors from two state medical societies said that 10 percent was the more realistic figure for doctor-related alcoholism. Indeed, the state medical society of Illinois physicians reported in *Med-*

ical World News that 11 percent of U.S. physicians were addicted to alcohol or drugs.

Estimates of the prevalence of incompetent physicians also vary, depending on the definition of "incompetence." Matthew Lifflander, director of the Medical Practice Task Force set up by the New York State Assembly in 1977, estimated the number of incompetent physicians "conservatively at fifteen percent," and that "as many as twenty-five percent are incompetent to do some of the things they do."

Dr. Robert Erwin Jones, associate medical director of the Institute of the Pennsylvania Hospital, a psychiatric clinic in Philadelphia, reviewed the case histories of one hundred doctors admitted from 1967 to 1975. Jones said the percentage of those diagnosed to be alcoholic or mentally ill may be understated because doctors attending doctors hate to stick their colleagues with such potentially damaging labels as "alcoholic" or "schizophrenic," which might lead to loss of license. Jones said that although drug abuse appeared as the primary diagnosis in only 12 percent of the cases, the doctors' medical records showed 52 percent of them had a significant alcohol or drug problem. In another study conducted in 1967, Dr. Modlin, the Menninger Foundation psychiatrist, and a fellow researcher investigated drug addiction among physicians and found the problem so severe—30 percent to 100 percent higher than that for the general population—that it could be classified as an "occupational hazard." To which the AMA added, "The problem of the impaired physician is a complicated one, both legally and ethically, but it is a challenge that can no longer be ignored."

Nor do psychiatrists get off any easier. Dr. Modlin, who is a professor of community and forensic psychiatry at the Menninger Foundation, feels that the odds of a psychiatrist committing suicide are more than 50 percent higher than those for the average American. Psychiatrists, he said, have the highest suicide rate in the medical profession.

Why? This is so because of the nature of their work. "We therapists keep too much to ourselves," he wrote in the *Menninger Perspective* magazine. "Instead of consulting with colleagues, we indulge in self-supervision, self-counseling and self-treatment."

A pattern starts to become obvious. Somewhere on his way to becoming master of his art, the doctor who is imbalanced or prone to suicide has failed to learn the rudiments of living. It is plain that doctors must realize they are only human, that medicine is an art, that a great deal of what leads a man to his sickbed, and then out of it, is simply not known, and that medical people, like the rest of humankind, make mistakes and must be forgiven—most of all by themselves.

Ironically, it is because doctors are only human that not only do many of the alcoholics not only deny their affliction, but an alarming number of them are repelled by it in others. "Physicians are only human," says Dr. John Erwin, psychiatrist and alcoholism researcher, in *Medical World News*. "At times the physician's patience is tried and wears thin. At times, indeed, somewhere inside there may be a little voice crying faintly for the same forbidden pleasures of regressive infantilism permitted the sick patient. At such times, the defense is often that of projection. He says, in effect: 'It is not I, the physician, who wishes to be taken care of and to wallow in self-pity. I am strong and self-controlled. He is weak and lacking in control. See how he indulges himself by drinking too much. I cannot imagine such tendencies in myself. Indeed, I will prove this by venting my rage upon anyone who gives in like this.' "

This does not apply solely to doctors who are alcoholic

but also to those who are "social drinkers," who occasionally overindulge and have reason to be suspicious about their drinking. I discussed this point with Hinsdale San's Dr. Charles Anderson, a teetotaler. He explained that "doctors who drink are too often cruel toward alcoholics because they see themselves in alcoholics and they think: 'This is what I could be, or may be. Maybe this is what I'm slowly heading for. Maybe I'm almost there and I haven't realized it.' And there follows a resentment toward the alcoholic, and sometimes that resentment becomes an aversion. My alcoholic patients have often told me there is no question but that the teetotaling physician is more sympathetic and understanding of the alcoholic."

Dr. Nelson Bradley, who has spent a lifetime studying the disease, has this view: "The biggest problem in alcoholism diagnosis is the reluctance of our culture to accept the diagnosis of alcoholism. Those members of the American Medical Association who find it difficult to face up to this diagnosis or are even reluctant to discuss it with their patients are as unexplainable as a physician who continues to ignore an elevated temperature or vacillates over a right lower quadrant pain. It is a thing of wonder that the disciplined man of medicine has found himself walking along with the social pathology that so fastidiously tries to deny or reject this awful presence. When presented with any other sort of medical symptoms, he attacks them with such efficiency and dispatch that he allows nothing to interfere with his pursuit. He disregards all the normal needs and apprehensions of the patient and thinks of the patient's other problems as mundane—so much so that the doctor not only develops the hallowed image of the dedicated and skilled physician, but also the image of a person who is arrogant, unaware of and unconcerned about the needs and feelings of his patients."

The denial of what Dr. Bradley described as "this awful presence" was dramatized the night I spent in the home of a Waukegan, Illinois, doctor, who denied the presence of alcoholism in himself but not in other sufferers. I was with my friend, Jim, who, with well-timed scoldings, was to revive a sort of waning interest in my own life. The doctor was living alone, and I remember being almost speechless as Jim scolded him: "You're blaming a woman for this, and you know that's a cop out. You're on the pity-pot, and you're going to have to get off your duff or you're going to die here in this pigpen. And you know something? Nobody's going to give a damn when you die."

I looked around. The home was in disarray and the doctor, a huge man, was sitting on the kitchen floor. He was in his underclothes, and in his hands he held a towel in which he kept coughing blood. There was blood on his chest and on his shorts. At this time he had reduced his practice to almost nothing—sometimes not answering his telephone for days.

On the way home I told Jim I did not see how the doctor was going to make it. But he later made a dramatic recovery—Jim kept taking him to AA meetings—and he has since told me that he was sure he had been just mere days from death. But en route home from the doctor's house that night, what kept running through my mind were Jim's words to the bloody hulk on the floor:

"Nobody's going to give a damn when you die."

THIRTEEN

The incidents that follow are related not to demean or criticize alcoholism counselors. I cite them to alert problem drinkers considering treatment that they will run into some counselors whom they will find incompetent or offensive. The competent, compassionate counselors are in the majority—and I have known many. Except for a few, they are able, dedicated people—most of them recovered alcoholics who "have been there," and they are devoted to helping those who trudge the road of endless agony and for whom life is mostly the lonely, desolate interval between midnight and dawn. They have assigned themselves the task of easing the terrors of the people they once were, because they know the suffering involved as few nonalcoholic healers know it, and because counseling helps maintain their own sobriety.

But just as there are mediocre lawyers, plumbers, accountants and newsmen, there are inept and unfit alcoholism counselors. This, however, should not frighten away the problem drinker from seeking treatment even if he is occasionally disappointed or discouraged in his quest for sobriety. I was hurt—even scared—more than once, but I remain grateful for what several counselors have done for me and will always value their friendship.

One counselor who almost caused me to lose faith held

sway at one of the first treatment centers I attended. A pompous man, he told me one morning to go to the medical unit of the hospital for a blood test. I found this curious, because I had been in the hospital for two weeks and had had all the regular tests. It happened that my wife was on hand for a family conference after lunch, and the first thing he said when we walked into his office was, "I suppose you're wondering why you got another blood test this morning." I said I had wondered about it. He said, "It's because I think you're drinking."

"Drinking? Here?"

"Yes."

At first I had the uneasy feeling that this was some psychological ploy to test my reaction under anger. But I knew blood would not have been drawn from my arm for the sake of a psychogenic experiment. Besides, the look on his face was dead serious.

"I haven't had a drink since before I came here," I protested.

"I think someone brought you a bottle, or maybe you're sneaking out to a bar."

"I tell you I haven't had a drink!" I said, my voice rising. It was bad enough to be accused of drinking in treatment, which usually meant instant dismissal, but to hear this in front of my wife was a huge embarrassment. The more I denied it, the more flustered I became, and the look on the face of my wife, who had heard my denials so often before, made me want to go for the counselor's throat. My frustration was such that I was stammering.

"Why are you doing this?" I said. "Why won't you believe me?"

He brought his fingertips together and I remembered that suddenly the look in his eyes brought just one word to my mind: cobra.

"The blood test will tell," he said. "It'll be up at four."

My wife agreed to wait until four, and we sat in the lobby, she mostly expressing silent resignation. The two-hour wait was a torment. Was it possible there was still alcohol in my bood after two weeks? And if it was, how could I continue to proclaim my innocence?

"You have to believe me," I told her. "I would never do that in a place like this. I came here to stop drinking."

And I was even frantic enough to pray, "Please, it can't really be, can it?"

At 4 P.M. my wife and I were called into the counselor's office again. He was in a swivel chair, staring out the window. He did not greet us as we took our seats. Worse, he sat in silence with his back to us, gazing at a gathering storm. Finally he swiveled around and brought the tips of his fingers together.

"Negative," he said simply.

Because of my agitation, I couldn't feel relieved. "That means it shows I haven't been drinking," I said.

"The test is negative. No alcohol."

"That means I haven't been drinking?" I thought the repetition sounded stupid.

"It means there's no evidence you've been drinking."

"No explanation? No apology?"

"Apology?"

"Look, you didn't ask if I'd been drinking. You said you thought I was, and you sent me for a blood test to prove it. You made me sweat it out here with my wife for hours. And all you've got to say is 'negative.' Don't you think you owe me an explanation?"

"It was a hunch I had. Now let's get on to other things."

Since then, this man has found employment at four other treatment centers (including a hospital where a fe-

male counselor was fired after it was discovered that she
was addicted to pills).

In the treatment center of another hospital, something
of a similar nature—but worse—happened to me in the
presence of about twenty-five patients. Again it involved a
false accusation, but this time the accusation involved taking pills, though the type of pills was never spelled out.
(This attitude—a blend of blunt allegation and studied
vagueness—is what prompts me to use terms like "medioc-
rity" and "ineptness," to describe behavior that borders on
the dangerous.)

On this occasion we were assembled in a unit group. The
head counselor waded right in: "Paul, will you tell the
group where you are getting your pills?"

"What pills?"

"I think you're on pills."

"You're kidding!"

"I'm serious. I think you're taking pills."

I looked around. Most of the group seemed astonished. I
had been in the hospital about ten days and most of them
had come to know me. Naturally I was stunned because, as
I have stated earlier, I not only have never taken pills (except in a hospital), I have a decided fear of them (probably
because I had read so much about the deadly consequences
of mixing them with alcohol). Since I even hold aspirin at
a distance, the counselor's charge was almost laughable.
Yet it was far from funny, because I recalled too bitterly
the previous accusation of drinking made by the "cobra."
This time I exploded. I slapped my hand on a nearby table
(with such force that I felt the sting for two days), then
stood up and paced the floor like a lawyer addressing a jury.
But this was not a pleading; it was an outburst:

"A couple of years ago I was accused of drinking while
in a place like this. I was never told why, even after submit-

ting to a blood test that proved negative. Now it's pills. For God's sake, I don't even know what color an upper or a downer or whatever you call those things is. I don't even know what a marijuana cigarette looks like. What's going on here?"

"Your general attitude," replied the counselor, a squat, bearded man. "You don't mix. You spend your spare time alone."

"I mix at all the sessions and in the dining room. In my spare time I read the books and pamphlets you people give us when we check in here. I happen to be a loner, but if my attitude is what makes you think I take pills, then you better do some reading yourself. You call that a reason? I think you're an idiot!"

At this point I was striding up and down the room, pausing occasionally in front of the counselor to shout at him. I was breathing hard, and so was he. There was an ashtray near his feet, and I kicked it halfway across the room, again shouting:

"If I'm on pills, why don't you send me out now for a blood test or a urine test? I'm not afraid. Why don't you order the test right now? Are you afraid? I think you are!"

The counselor then addressed the group: "Ladies and gentlemen, I leave it to you. You've observed Paul these past few days. Do any of you care to comment?"

Five or six did, and all said they had noticed nothing unusual about me. The counselor seemed unimpressed. "It's not just your attitude," he said. "I've noticed you walk funny."

"Walk funny? I've been getting Valium four times a day for over a week! Valium's got some of these people here bouncing off the walls. That's the only drug I've had in me, and that's been ordered by your doctors. What kind of bullshit is this?"

Then came a non sequitur which infuriated me all the more. "Just because you're a celebrity," the counselor said, "doesn't give you the right to be a recluse and shun your peers."

"I don't know what you're talking about," I said. "I just don't know what you're talking about."

At this point a short, balding man stood up. He was an assistant producer at a midwestern television station.

"I've got a question for Paul," he said, turning to me. "You're a columnist and you cover show business and you're in Hollywood and New York a lot, and you know all these show people, and you mean to tell me you don't know what uppers and downers look like?"

"You're damned right I don't."

"Well, I'm in television and I know some show biz people, and I know they take pills. So I don't believe you when you say you don't know what a joint looks like."

The counselor had pulled the celebrity bit on me, and this inane observation from the fat little producer gave me my chance. I marched up to him and said:

"Look, I was in Hollywood a little while back and in one week I had dinner in Bob Hope's home, I spent an afternoon with Red Skelton in his pool, I was entertained by Dinah Shore in her home, I went to Mass one Sunday morning with Danny Thomas, I was at a party in Lucille Ball's home and I had drinks with George Gobel on his patio—and I never saw one damned pill or even heard talk of pills. Who are your friends in show business? Potheads who have to get stoned to perform?"

Incredibly, the counselor praised the producer for his opinion that people in show business had to be addicted to drugs. "I tend to agree with him," he said, which I interpreted as an endorsement of his charge against me.

"You haven't said anything about my request for a urine

test or any test," I said. "Surely you had my room and belongings searched. Yet you persist in this ridiculous accusation. If it's true, then why don't you have me thrown out of here? That's the usual procedure, isn't it? Why don't you? Is it because you'll have to answer to your bosses for losing the $175 a day it's costing me here?"

I paused for air, walked to my chair, turned toward the counselor again and said, "I have two things to say to you. First, you are the all-time, all-American son of a bitch. Second, you're a disgrace to your profession and a danger to the patients."

The wrangle had taken up the entire session, and the counselor adjourned the group for lunch. I happened to be in the same elevator with him, along with a couple of other counselors and some patients, and here I did something that was both laughable and silly. From my pocket I removed a packet of Tic Tacs, a small, capsule-shaped mint. "I've been taking these for years," I said, pouring them into my hand. "Is this what started this whole business?"

"Ha!" the counselor rumbled. "Nobody who's innocent would use a defense like Tic Tacs."

His strained logic shook me so much the Tic Tacs slipped out and clattered to the floor like a miniature hailstorm. The elevator door opened and the passengers stepped out, some of them giving me strange stares. I had overreacted, but my state of mind had made it impossible to underreact.

After lunch I went to my room, packed my bags and telephoned a friend to come and get me. He persuaded me to stay, which I did, but it was not a productive stay because my mind was no longer concentrating on the treatment. The four-week stay turned into a waste of time. It was also a waste of more than five thousand dollars, and when I left the hospital I stayed away from AA meetings

for two months. I was, of course, punishing no one but myself. That, sadly, is typical of the "stinking thinking" of
the alcoholic.

But my most shattering encounter was with a female
counselor who apparently had more of a fixation on oral
sex than a concern for sobriety. Surprisingly, on my day of
arrival at this hospital, the male counselor who briefed our
little band of new patients declared, in part:

"Now, we know that after four weeks here, male patients go into the women's rooms; and we know that female patients go into the men's rooms; and we also know
that some women go into other women's rooms. But that
isn't our main concern here; our main concern is to help
you attain sobriety."

I remember wondering at the time why he didn't sketch
the whole picture and suggest that some male patients
might visit other men's rooms. But the disturbing thought
was that he almost appeared to be condoning this behavior. For disoriented, befuddled first timers to treatment,
the speech was, at the very least, unnerving.

At the first meeting I had with my female counselor, the
first question she asked was whether my wife attended Al-
Anon meetings. (Al-Anon is a fellowship for relatives and
friends of alcoholics who meet to solve their common problems of fear, insecurity, lack of understanding of the alcoholic and of the warped relationships associated with alcoholism.) I told her my wife had attended one Al-Anon
meeting, hadn't liked it, and never returned.

"So," the counselor snapped, "you blame your wife for
your drinking?"

"I said nothing of the kind. I just said she doesn't go to
Al-Anon."

There was a long pause, after which she said, "You're
here under false pretenses, aren't you?"

"What do you mean?"

"You're here to write an article about us, aren't you?"

"No, I'm not."

"A few years ago you wrote one, didn't you?"

"Yes, I wrote an anonymous magazine article a year after I was in treatment in a hospital. And it happened to be very favorable to the hospital. What's that got to do with my being here now?"

Another long pause occurred, and then she asked, "What do you think of homosexuality?"

"Is that relevant?"

"Do you think homosexuality is a sickness, like alcoholism?"

"No, I don't."

"You condone alcoholism, but you don't condone homosexuality?"

"I don't condone either. Where are we going with this conversation, anyway?"

"What have you got against homosexuals?"

"Hey, I didn't say I had anything against them. But it just doesn't happen to be my bag."

"Why is alcoholism not so bad, but homosexuality is bad?"

"You're comparing the two, ma'am, and I don't see any comparison."

The woman looked away for a short time and then said, "What do you think of oral sex?"

"For God's sake, what has this got to do with my drinking problem?"

"Do you indulge in oral sex?"

"Again, I think that's irrelevant, and besides, it's none of your business. If it is, why don't you ask me tomorrow in group session?"

"Do you and your wife have oral sex?"

"If you think I'm going to tell you—"

"Does your wife object to it?"

I stood up. "I'm leaving," I said. "Not just your office. I'm leaving this place. I think you're a sick woman."

As I got to the door, she said, "You know that if you leave the hospital before a certain number of days your insurance won't cover you for the time you were here. I'm going to have to report this to your insurance people and you're going to have to pay the whole thing."

"Go to hell!" I said, and I slammed the door.

I called the office of Dr. Mike, the alcoholic physician whom the Hinsdale San's Dr. Anderson had originally sent to see me, together with my friend, Jim. He was vacationing in Florida and it took me hours to reach him. When I did, I spilled out the whole story of my confrontation with the counselor.

"This is awful," Dr. Mike said. "Get out of that hospital, and get out now. Don't worry about the insurance business. I'll talk with the hospital authorities when I get back and I'll see to it that you don't get screwed on your insurance coverage. But get out of there!"

I did. Within two hours I had discharged myself and was in a taxi. But I didn't go home. And I didn't go to an AA meeting.

I went to the Drake Oak Brook Hotel in Oak Brook, a wealthy suburb that adjoins Hinsdale. The Drake Oak Brook Hotel, progeny of the stately Drake Hotel in Chicago, is run by James A. Bailey almost as well as God runs the world. Bailey, executive vice president and general manager, was consistently an understanding and discreet person, but above all he was a gentle man.

It was at the Drake Oak Brook that I often retired, after drinking, when I was too ashamed or dysfunctional to go home. It seemed to lessen my guilt because I would hear so many "horror stories" from fellow drinkers in Chicago who would tell me they'd awaken in Denver or Albuquerque never knowing how they'd gotten there. Such awful things generally didn't happen to *me*. I was not the type who woke up thousands of miles from home unaware of how I'd gotten there. I'd simply wake up in the Drake Oak Brook—twenty minutes from my home.

In any event, after I'd stormed out of the hospital, I stayed at the Drake Oak Brook ten days—drinking, reading, thinking and drinking.

I was still a long, long way from surrender.

FOURTEEN

One day in 1976 I wrote to then President Gerald Ford, asking him to help me with a project for alcoholics. In one of those curious turns of events, I received a reply from his wife, Betty, who two years later was to stun the world with the announcement that she was an alcoholic and was about to enter a treatment center.

The project involved a picnic for members of AA and their families, sponsored by a halfway house in a midwestern city where, now legally separated from my wife, I was living. Halfway houses are a kind of poor relative in the scheme of government assistance, always in need of money to pay the rent and buy groceries. I suggested that we enliven the picnic with a drawing for prizes to raise funds and undertook to ask show business and sports celebrities I knew to donate prizes—personal things such as a tie, an item used in a movie or an autographed baseball. In each letter I specifically asked my friends not to send a check but some personal possession that would give the drawing a little glamor.

Bob Hope, for example, sent a silver cigarette lighter featuring the famed "ski nose" profile. Unfortunately, it was such a hit that it was pilfered by one of the halfway house directors and never did make it to the drawing. Also "liberated" before the picnic was a bumper supply of hot dogs wangled from the head of a meat-packing firm. An alcoholic resident, evidently not yet recovered, made off with the meat in the dead of night, which suggests that life in a halfway house is something less than Shangri-la. On a happier note, William Nail, public relations director for Zenith Radio Corporation, donated a magnificent color television set which eventually replaced the broken-down monstrosity in the institution, which hadn't had a clear picture since the days of "Howdy Doody."

As a newsman accustomed to going to the top, I decided to ask President Ford for a donation. I told him what we were trying to accomplish as alcoholics and asked if he would donate a pen he had used to sign some bill or other, which would be the drawing's *pièce de résistance*. I ended the letter with the following sentence: "Send anything, Mr. President, but don't send booze to us boozers." In view of the First Lady's drinking problem, which was not publicly known at the time, he must have winced at what I had intended as a mild joke.

In due time a package arrived from Washington. It contained a presidential pen, together with a letter from Mrs. Ford, who explained that her husband was out of the country and she was replying in his stead. Since it was a letter from the White House, I made it a part of the grand prize, so I don't remember her exact words. But it was a gracious letter. She praised the work we were doing in combating the "critical" problem of alcoholism.

Little did I realize that later she would do so much in the battle against the disease by openly admitting her own alcoholism (as have an increasing number of personalities in the public eye).

In her autobiography *The Times of My Life*, Mrs. Ford explained that it was the intervention of her children that finally persuaded her to enter Long Beach Naval Hospital for alcoholism treatment. "Some doctors responded well to the training," she wrote. "Some responded badly. There was one who was very unsympathetic. 'I resent being waked up at three o'clock in the morning to have to go and detox an alcoholic,' he said. We didn't let him get away with that. 'What if the patient had cancer or diabetes?' someone asked. 'Well, that would be different,' he said. We told him it wasn't different. Addiction is a sickness, a terminal sickness; it can be arrested by abstinence, but there is no cure for the disease.

"At first, I loathed the [group therapy] sessions. I was uncomfortable, unwilling to speak up. Then one day another woman said she didn't think that drinking was a problem, and I became very emotional. I got to my feet. 'I'm Betty,' I said. 'I'm an alcoholic, and I know my drinking has hurt my family.' I heard myself, and I couldn't believe it. I was trembling; another defense had cracked.

"The reason I had rejected the idea that I was alcoholic was that my addiction wasn't dramatic. So my speech had become deliberate. So I forgot a few telephone calls. So I fell in the bathroom and cracked three ribs. But I never drank for a hangover . . . I hadn't been a solitary drinker, either; I'd never hidden bottles in the chandeliers or the toilet tanks . . . There had been no broken promises (my husband never came to me and said, 'please quit') and no drunken driving.

"In the end, what it comes down to is you have to take the responsibility for yourself. Never mind that your wife kept a dirty house, or your mother didn't like you, or your husband can't remember your wedding anniversary. Everybody's had disappointments, and anyone can rationalize his actions. . . . Blaming other people for your condition is a total waste of time."

The former First Lady kept a diary while in the hospital.

One night she wrote, "What in hell am I doing here?" When I read that I remembered those were almost precisely the same words I had used in a hospital several years ago.

The alcoholism treatment center at Long Beach Naval Hospital has seen many prominent individuals come and go, including Georgia Senator Herman E. Talmadge and Billy Carter, the President's brother, who said, "I feel so damn good. The hardest thing to do was to admit I was an alcoholic. I am an alcoholic. I'm cured as long as I don't take a drink. If I take a drink, I'm not cured anymore. And I found out water can be drank straight."

Why do so many people in powerful positions have drinking problems? Dr. Morris Chafetz, who helped create the National Institute on Alcohol Abuse and Alcoholism, has said that power, in and of itself, is intoxicating, and people who enjoy the power "high" tend to lean toward other intoxicating mechanisms.

"There are other reasons," he adds. "Powerful people are constantly courted with parties and socializing, and are frequently put into heavy drinking situations. Many powerful people also get into trouble with alcohol because they need heavy doses to relieve the mental and physical tensions of power. A member of Congress once said publicly: 'There is no better training ground for alcoholism than serving in the Congress of the United States.' His statement does not mean we are being served in Congress only by alcoholically ill people, but that frequent and heavy drinking is an occupational hazard of a power center like Congress."

During Richard Nixon's presidency, his domestic affairs adviser, John D. Ehrlichman, turned an embarrassing spotlight on the issue while testifying before the Senate Watergate Committee. "You can go over here in the Gallery," he said, "and watch a member totter onto the Floor in a condition of at least partial inebriation."

Former Representative Wilbur Mills was among those who came to know the hazards. "One of the great things about alcoholics is that we are great con artists. This is especially true of [those of] us who become alcoholic while in politics. It is necessary that we always cover up from those we ask to be our supporters. I would never let anybody know of the egotism that existed within myself. I knew that none of the other members of the [Ways and Means] Committee could handle legislation as well as I could. Why? Because God Himself, so many times, had asked me to take His place on the throne. And during the time that He allowed me to remain there, the world was free of wars. Not when He was running it, but when I was running it.

"I knew I wasn't an alcoholic. Members of Congress don't become alcoholics. Important, educated people don't become alcoholics. I found out I was wrong. In 1974, I was finally finding it necessary to take a drink in the morning before I could shave. Do you know that it is possible to cut your face with an electric razor? I learned how to do it. I became an expert at it. Toward the end of my drinking I got to the point where I did not want ice cubes in my glass, so I kept my booze in the icebox. I had a problem about drinking alcohol with ice cubes. What would happen if I swallowed one of those ice cubes? I might strangle. So I was drinking it straight. That was my way of drinking. I really had no problems with it. I could drink when I wanted to. I could quit drinking for months at a time, and I did. It never dawned on me that I was growing into alcoholism. I knew nothing about it. Now [after treatment] I think I am very fortunate. My sobriety comes as a gift from God. My ability to stay sober is due to God through other people.

The fact that I've done what they've told me to do, that
I've tried to be comfortable, that I've tried to be happy in
my sobriety, is a credit to others. I received a gift from a
power greater than I."

The power of politics also had an insidious effect on former Iowa Senator Harold Hughes, now a full-time gospel
worker. "The people I hurt most," he noted, "were my
wife, my children and my parents. My wife left me a number of times. Once I was so drunk I looked out the window
the next morning and couldn't find my car. I thought
maybe I had killed somebody. And I thought the only way
to break the cycle was to kill myself. I loaded my gun, lay
on the bed and put the barrel in my mouth. And then I
thought what a mess I'll leave in the bedroom, the room
that had meant so much in my marriage. I couldn't do that
to my wife, so I decided I'll go into the bathroom instead.
There, I thought maybe if there is a God, I should pray. I
told Him that if there was any reason for me to live, He
should take over my life, otherwise let me die. Suddenly, I
had a great feeling of peace. I unloaded the gun and went
to bed. That was twenty-seven years ago. I didn't have a
drink for two years, and I never drank again after that."

As husbands move forward in public life, many wives
feel left out and their drinking shifts from social to compulsive. Joy Baker, wife of Tennessee Senator Howard H.
Baker, Jr., said that she "fell apart" when her father, Senator Everett Dirksen, died. "They say life begins at forty.
Ha-ha. Forty was not a good year for me. Everybody was
doing something but me. I was forty, and where was I
going but down? I went all the way. I was rebellious. I was
belligerent. I was mixed up. I was mad at myself, my doctor, my husband, the bottle."

Marianne Brickley, who was once married to the lieuten-
ant governor of Michigan and is now the mother of six,

told a meeting of the National Council on Alcoholism, "A man calls his wife 'the little woman,' and too often that is exactly the way she feels. While my husband was climbing his political ladder to success, the only changing I did was of diapers. Trying to ease my frustrations, I graduated from beer to martinis. I became an alcoholic."

One of the most prominent alcoholics on the Washington scene was Joan Kennedy, who has moved from the capital to Boston, living separately from her husband, Senator Ted Kennedy. She stated in a *McCall's* magazine interview with Joan Braden that she didn't want to blame Washington for everything, "but I certainly was not comfortable going to AA and getting help in Washington. One of the most marvelous things about being in Boston is the privacy. I go to AA in Boston and it's wonderful. I can walk in, and there's no big flutter or whatever, and I'm just like any other person who is an alcoholic and who needs help to stay sober.

"I drank socially at first, and then I began to drink alcoholically. I really did. But at the time I didn't know it. No one really ever does know. But it is so insidious that you don't really think about it as it is happening. For the moment, it blots out reality. It blots out a lot of things that you don't really want to look at. I think many people drink because they're unhappy or because they're under great stress, because they don't feel they fit in or they are unhappy with their lives or themselves, too. Whatever it was, I began to feel upset with myself. And I think there's a terrible stigma attached to drinking too much or being an alcoholic. And most especially, and unfortunately, this stigma is much worse for a woman. And so I did what a lot of Americans do who have a drinking problem—they begin to try to hide it out of shame and to pretend it's not as bad a problem as it really is.

"I tried to talk about it, but I was embarrassed and Ted was embarrassed, but nobody would really talk about it. Even my best friends would tiptoe around it. I suppose they were trying to protect me. They didn't want to hurt my feelings. And so I continued to drink more and more. And the situation got progressively worse. And I tried seeing a psychiatrist. I must say a lot of people in the medical profession in this country really don't know much about alcoholism. And so I really got no help there. I tried, and when I gave that up I really didn't know where to turn.

"People ask whether the newspaper stories about Ted and girls hurt my feelings. Of course they hurt my feelings. They went to the core of my self-esteem. When one grows up feeling that maybe one is sort of special and hoping that one's husband thinks so, and then suddenly thinking maybe he doesn't . . . Well, I didn't lose my self-esteem altogether, but it was difficult to hear all the rumors. And I began thinking, well, maybe I'm just not attractive enough or attractive any more, or whatever, and it was awfully easy to then say, 'Well, after all, you know, if that's the way it is, I might as well have a drink.' It wasn't my personality to make a lot of noise. Or to yell or scream or do anything. My personality was more shy and retiring. And so rather than get mad, or ask questions concerning the rumors about Ted and his girl friends, or really stand up for myself at all, it was easier for me to just go and have a few drinks and calm myself down as if I weren't hurt or angry. I didn't know how to deal with it. And, unfortunately, I found out that alcohol could sedate me. So I didn't care as much. And things didn't hurt so much."

Mrs. Kennedy also told Joan Braden in the McCall's interview that besides attending AA she sees a psychiatrist three times a week and no longer drinks at all. "Occasionally I miss it," she admitted, "because it had become a physical and psychological addiction. But I finally decided there is one thing in my life that I didn't need and that was drinking. So I stopped drinking, and it wasn't until then that I wanted to find out why I had been drinking and also try to figure out more about me so that, God forbid, I wouldn't want to go back to drinking. The better I know myself, the less chance there is that I would do anything like that. And the healthier person I would be without using any chemical in my life. I am exceptionally happy in my sobriety."

Another recovered alcoholic, actress Jan Clayton, famed as the mother in the "Lassie" movies and television series, echoed one of Mrs. Kennedy's thoughts, but in blunter terms. Speaking at the national convention of the Association of Labor and Management Administrators and Consultants on Alcoholism in San Diego in 1976, she said, "If a man 'ties on one,' so to speak, at a party, 'wasn't he a caution? Wasn't he a card? And didn't that lampshade look adorable on him? But did you see his wife? Wasn't she disgusting?' Because that is the word society most often tacks on to a drinking woman—disgusting. The hand that rocks the cradle is not supposed to hold a drink on the rocks. It's that damn pedestal, not of our making, not of our wanting. It places us beyond hearing or calling for help, way out of reach, and so the woman stays hidden, shamed and shamefully, in that 'closet in the sky' too often until everything is lost—her job, her family, and finally her life."

The female sense of inadequacy suggested here is reflected in the feelings of another public luminary, Joyce Burditt, a programing executive for the ABC television station in Hollywood and author of *The Cracker Factory*. "I just couldn't cope with my responsibilities. Things like dirty dishes, three small, bratty kids, toys scattered around the living room and dust on the TV set just drove me to drink. I started drinking after I became a housewife and mother. I felt very young and inadequate. I'd go to the market, for example, and look at all the other women shopping and think, 'They're all perfect homemakers and I'm a klutz,' and I'd run home and drink. I was so self-pitying it was unbelievable. But if there's one thing I learned it's that you have to stop worrying about who stole your little red wagon when you were three years old. The reality is everyone's little red wagon is stolen sometime. After joining AA, I was sure it was nothing but a group of winos. But I found out differently. I saw some of my neighbors there, people I'd seen before in department stores and churches. I said to a woman who I thought was a real pillar of the community, 'My God, I thought you were perfect.' She said, 'Well, I am perfect. It's just that I have this disease.' The stigma of alcoholism is particularly hard on a woman. It's as if she belongs in the gutter or something. It takes courage to admit you're an alcoholic, and I think more women are getting that courage."

One of the first female celebrities to find that courage was actress Mercedes McCambridge, who publicly admitted her alcoholism in 1968. She still has mixed feelings about it:

"I'm sorry 40 per cent, 50 per cent of the time that I ever spoke out. Do you realize that in the next presidential race there could be three candidates married to women who have had problems with alcohol—Ted Kennedy, Gerald Ford and Howard Baker? That tells you something about the extent of the problem. But do you think people in the wind-washed Bible Belt of America will accept that fact? Don't you think they will tell themselves, 'Do I want a woman like that as First Lady?' and decide they don't. I have been the subject of terrible hate mail. When I walk into a studio, into most any place during the last ten years, the first thing that hits me is that everyone knows I'm a reformed alcoholic, that that's the first thing they think of when they see me. It hurts."

Something akin to the opposite happened to Dick Van Dyke when he "went public" with his alcoholism. "There was a lot of shock from it, and of course I got a lot of mail, but I didn't get one negative note from anybody—to this day." This strengthens the theory that a double standard does exist in the public's reaction to male and female alcoholism.

Van Dyke, whose wife is also a recovered alcoholic, is convinced he was physically addicted to alcohol. "Alcoholism is an absolute physical addiction and once someone begins to drink continuously it is usually because his body needs alcohol to function. There's no such thing as an alcoholic personality, a personality disposed toward addiction. There is no moral weakness, no character lack involved. I think the chances of becoming alcoholic depend entirely on whether you are physiologically addicted or not. Especially in my business. I have friends who drink heavily every day. They have three martinis at lunch, and they may drink during the afternoon. But they're not alcoholics."

Van Dyke said that going to a treatment center in a hospital was "probably the smartest move I ever made in my life. It's an unbelievable feeling. I can only describe it as being born again."

Does he ever get the urge to drink again? "It's unbelievably hard. You don't realize how much of a craving you have. But if you think 'I can never drink again,' you won't make it. It has to be a day-to-day thing. I have to keep remembering that alcoholism is a neurophysiological disease. In fact, scientists have proved that the glands, the heart, the liver, even the brain cells of an alcoholic undergo changes, so that they actually derive their energy from the calories in alcohol. The body craves it. At the same time, although alcohol acts as a depressant for the social drinker, it's a stimulant for an alcoholic. He needs it to live."

As more and more public figures reveal themselves as victims of the disease and discuss the results of their treatment, I believe that more and more alcoholics suffering in secrecy will emerge into the open, drop their shame and realize that their situation is not only not hopeless, it is not helpless. It is my own feeling that within a decade or so the word "anonymous," where alcoholism is concerned, may become obsolete.

If this sounds like an overestimation, one need only hark back ten or twelve years, when emotional problems and mental breakdowns were spoken of only in whispers. Today most people discuss such ailments much as they compare notes on ulcers and sore backs. And being "in analysis" or seeing a psychiatrist is not only commonplace but has almost become a status symbol.

FIFTEEN

It was only after my marriage came apart and I was living alone, thinking, that I realized I was not the only one at home with a drinking problem. All of my eight children had one, too. And so did my wife.

My estranged wife is a social drinker, and the children—through what good fortune I'll never know—show little inclination to drink. But they have a drinking problem because the people around an alcoholic are vulnerable. Children, especially, sense that something is wrong, but since they do not fully understand what is going on—that the alcoholic father is projecting his own lack of self-esteem—they frequently feel as much guilt as he does. "What did I do to cause this?" they ask themselves. "Would it be better if I weren't around? If I hadn't been born?"

Recalling her feelings as a sixteen-year-old high schooler, my daughter, Marcia, now a twenty-four-year-old married registered nurse, said in a group therapy session at the Hinsdale San, "When I was introduced by the teachers and people like that, I was always introduced as the daughter of Paul Molloy, the author and columnist, not as Marcia Molloy. And it was the oddest feeling. In a way, I was proud, but then I would think, 'If only they knew—dad's been drinking for days and they're using his name to introduce me.' I was sad and puzzled about this because, inside,

I knew it was something like, well, hypocrisy. It was confusing and sometimes it actually made me sick because I knew dad didn't hate us, he hated himself. There was no hatred for us coming through, but his suffering, his low self-esteem, that came through. There was a lot of hurt, broken promises, and sometimes I didn't know if I should bring my friends home because there was a lot of mood changing, mood shifting. I didn't know whether he would be a real nice drunk today or a mean one."

Vernon E. Johnson, founder of the nonprofit Johnson Institute in Minneapolis, put it this way: "Out of feelings of guilt, the victims of the alcoholic's projection become emotionally distressed, often as severely as the chemically dependent person himself. This means that every sick alcoholic is surrounded by sick non-alcoholics."

Johnson, who is on the faculty of The School of Alcohol Studies of the universities of Georgia, North Dakota, and Rutgers University, adds, "The people around the alcoholic have predictable experiences that are psychologically damaging. As they meet failure after failure, their feelings of fear, frustration, shame, inadequacy, guilt, resentment, self-pity and anger mount, and so do their defenses. They, too, use rationalization as a defense against these feelings, because they are threatened with a growing sense of self-worthlessness. Their defenses have begun to operate in the same way as the alcoholic's, although they are not conscious of this, and they are also victimized by their defenses rather than helped. Out of touch with reality, just like the alcoholic, they say, 'I don't need help. It's his problem, not mine!' The chemically dependent and those around him all have impaired judgment; they differ only in the degree of impairment. They, too, need real help and should be included in any therapy."

Marcia, some seven years after the fact, specifically re-

membered the night I missed her high school graduation.
"That really, really hurt," she said.

It hurt me, too, to hear it so much later because when
drinking episodes like that happened, I saw them only as
occasional incidents, something lamentable but that could
be forgotten because it would not happen again. My thinking was warped to the point where I did not see the overall
effect, the total consequence, just the isolated incidents.

"What hurt was that dad was wrapped up in his work
and the drinking," Marcia said. "We children were noticed
all right, but we weren't sought out. I was even mad at
mother because I felt, at the time, that she was doing nothing about it. What scared us more than his drinking was
his suffering. I used to think, 'He's got a good job and loves
his work. Why should he be so unhappy?' My big question
was always, 'God, we all love each other, so what's eating
him up?' Even when I got to understand, there were breaking points and then I'd get sick of it all.

"But I never gave up hope because he was always trying.
Every birthday, when I blew out the candles, my wish was
that he would stop drinking. Because we had such good
times and he was good to us when he wanted to be. He was
always a very funny man, so it wasn't a constant hell. The
deviant part is that we manipulated him when he drank;
like we could get the car, and money, or stay out late. But
we didn't like what we were doing. Anyway, there was always love and I guess that's why we survived."

I asked my eldest, Paul, Jr., now thirty-two and married,
about his feelings in those early years. "It brought an aloneness to us," he said. "But I was the oldest and you spent
more time with me. For instance, you were always at my
Little League games, but sometimes I'd notice you had
slipped away for an inning or two, and I figured it was for a
drink, so sometimes I wondered if you were using some of

the games to get out of the house for a few drinks. Sometimes I was too embarrassed to bring my friends home, and that made me mad, but you kept rebounding back, so there was never any love lost at any time.

"Sometimes when you were out of town I remember I'd worry that you might be drinking. But the way you kept picking yourself up—I think it gave me a new perspective on love, so I gained from that. By the time I left for college, my feeling was that you couldn't deal with the pressure of success. Actually, I didn't see much of your drinking, so it wasn't that big a deal, and I always felt that we'd make it all right."

Again, as in Marcia's high school incident, I was totally unaware that my ducking out of my son's baseball games now and then could have had such a profound effect on him at so tender an age.

Another of my daughters, Nelda, twenty-six, who has a bachelor's degree in psychology, said she first realized that something was "not quite right" when she was an eight-year-old third grader. "By the time I was in high school," she said, "I felt like we were all in a battle together, and we got scars. It felt like we were in the line of fire, but the fire wasn't necessarily aimed at us children individually. I resented your and mom's preoccupation with yourselves, the arguments, and felt there was not enough time for me. But then there were eight of us kids and it was hard to divide up the time.

"But though we'd tear at each other, we were close. The responsibility for survival was on each one, yet we were always trying to help each other out. We had a whole lot of contact with each other, and that was positive. There were heights and depths—lots of anger and lots of love, and that could be quite confusing. But we seemed to have a great support system.

"There were bad and good things. I learned to expect disappointment, like when you'd break a promise to take us somewhere. But learning to expect disappointment doesn't make it easier to bear. We were becoming young adults, and I know that sometimes I used you and the drinking as an excuse for not living up to my responsibilities. I think we all did. I had to change that, stop blaming your drinking for some of my own problems. But I feel that with responsibility we grew up faster. I learned early to make my own decisions, like my schooling, and this made me more capable, more independent. I learned compassion and sensitivity to others, and I became pretty perceptive of people. I feel I got an independence that most kids don't get, and that's terrific.

"You had an anesthetic for your pain, and we didn't. We did take advantage of you because discipline was erratic sometimes. But when things were good, they were very, very good. And we made it through, maybe because there was always humor in the house. It was rough at times, but we kept lots of respect and love for each other, and I think that's why we didn't disintegrate."

Georgia, thirty-one and the mother of two, said that when she was only ten she would steal my bottles and empty them into the kitchen sink. "I used to enjoy seeing you not drink for six or eight months," she said, "then you'd start again, and I'd wonder why, and empty the bottles.

"When I was in high school I didn't see too much of your drinking, because you'd be writing all night and off to work in the morning. It was only when I started in college that I noticed your drinking became psychotic.

"By that I mean when I was younger you seemed to be a happy drinker, but then the progressiveness made a change in your personality. The arguing between you and mom was what affected me the most, and so often I used to hope you'd get divorced. But I think we didn't come apart, and outlived all this, because we were looking out for each other."

The last three children—Mark, Barbara and Lisa—were born exactly within twenty-seven months of each other, so that Mark, the youngest, did not have, as he put it, "anyone to discuss it seriously with" in his younger years. "It was confusing," he said, "but somehow I thought this was the way all families lived. I wasn't scared of your drinking, just nervous over the arguing. But I really thought that was normal. When I got older I didn't think we'd fall apart because I knew what you were like when you were sober, and it was always fun. It's funny, but what I remember most was when the carnival or other attractions came to town. When you were sober, I knew I'd have two dollars, but when you were drinking you were good for at least five dollars. And I made sure I got it, and more.

"I went to Al-Ateen (similar to Al-Anon, but mainly intended for the children of alcoholics) a few times, but I wasn't impressed. I listened to their stories and I didn't feel I belonged there. I felt sorry for these kids because I figured their parents were drunken bums, but you had made a name for yourself. I just couldn't put my father at the low level of their fathers." (Incidentally, in his sophomore year at the University of Illinois Mark wrote his first college thesis for his rhetoric [writing] class, and got an A. The subject: alcoholism.)

This is an interesting (and eerie) comment, because it was precisely the same attitude I had when I first went to AA. It took me a long time to identify with its members; I held myself above them and found it both painful and difficult to blend into the fellowship because, I reasoned, they were *drunks* and I was an intelligent, educated man who simply *got drunk*.

When she was eighteen, my daughter Lisa, now a young mother, wrote me a letter when I was drying out in some hospital. I was so impressed by what she said (and, professionally, by her writing style) that I kept it. It read:

"I don't think I've ever written you a letter before, but I guess that doesn't matter. I've always felt more comfortable putting words down on paper anyway. What I want to say, and what I want you to know and believe, is this: I love you.

"I always have and I always will. When I was younger, your drinking problem didn't affect me as it does now. Before AA you were to me the man I had known since [I was] a baby. You were moody, irritable and scary. You quit drinking, seriously, with AA when I was in about seventh or eighth grade. And then I met my father. You didn't turn into a different man. You just showed me for the first time the man you really are. I don't know if you can understand this, but to me this is who you are:

"My father first, last and always. You are a warm person, full of life, lively and vivacious. You always have something good to say. You made me laugh and dinners were something I looked forward to more than anything all day. To be together, everyone, and with my father, I felt as though I had just met you even though you'd always been there for years.

"I have to admit I'm very fortunate. Had I always known the kind of man you are, I might have taken it for granted. But through your problems, I have grown. I love you. We all do more than you realize, I'm sure.

"When things get rough and you get sick, I may act as though I can't stomach you. But it's the drink that I hate, not the man swallowing it. It's a selfish hate, I know, but I can't help that. I'm being deprived of something I want—you—and that's selfish on my part.

"But what I want to say thru all this is that no matter what the future will be like, I'll always love you, and I'll always hate the drink. You're a fantastic guy, but then you're *my* father."

My daughter Shonagh, now twenty-nine, put it this way: "I certainly don't relish the old times—too many traumas. I don't know how it would have been if you didn't drink. Would life at home have been more peaceful? Up until about 1968 it was very hard living with you, and it's taken me a while to calm down. But now I'm very happy and feel in top shape and frame [of mind]."

And from Barbara, twenty-two and still at college: "I can't really remember any traumas. What I do remember is that the hardest time for me was when you were drinking and still unable to admit to yourself or to the family that you were an alcoholic. I knew that there was nothing that anyone could say or do that was going to keep you sober until you made that choice for yourself. All we could do was stand by and hope that you made that decision before it was too late to make any difference. Above all, I hated knowing I had no impact. It frustrated me to be so helpless. But I've never loved you any less and I don't remember ever really believing that you loved me any less because you drank. But I'd be lying if I said I didn't resent it. Drinking changed you. Whether it made you angry or clownish and sentimental, as it often did, whether it caused a fight or made you the life of the dinner table, I resented it because, no matter what your mood, when you were drunk you were a different person. When you were sober I used to say to myself, 'That's my father.' But when you were drunk you seemed to be an impostor. When it comes right down to it, though, I don't think your alcoholism had as many drastic effects as you might think. I can almost say that I've benefited from it in certain ways. I believe the whole family has. To make the transformation from an alcoholic who wouldn't be helped to an alcoholic who had the guts to admit that he needed it took a lot of honesty and strength. It took dedication and love on the part of the family. I just can't have too many regrets when I consider that I'm part of that family."

A significant thought runs throughout my children's comments. I purposely "interviewed" them separately, and each either mentioned or touched on "survival." This is something that never entered my mind when I was drinking during their growing-up years, yet it is obvious that survival, or the fear of not surviving, was paramount in their minds. I think it is the nature of alcoholics—certainly it was the nature of this alcoholic—to be unaware of such major matters as survival, or to blot them entirely out of their thinking.

My first book (*And Then There Were Eight*) had made the eight children very well known locally and nationally. I soon developed a fear that the recognition they achieved could be dangerous; I became almost paranoid about the risk (I imagined) of their being kidnapped. So I became extremely possessive of them and my drinking aggravated the situation. For long periods I was suspicious of their friends, of strangers who stopped to chat with us in restaurants and other public places, of business enterprises seeking their endorsement of products, and so on. Yet it was a bizarre protectiveness, somewhat like the wealthy woman who buys a costly diamond necklace and then keeps it out of sight in a vault. The love was there, yet often I felt a detachment. I'm not sure if this was genuine fear, or shame, or both, but I do feel that my drinking played a role in this twist of emotions. Part of the feeling—and this was constant with me—was that my alcoholism had placed them in jeopardy of the very curse in whose clutches I had strayed. But they are grown now, independent and responsible, and there is no sign that the sickness that was absent in the generation that preceded mine is present in the one that followed it. Whom can I thank for this but Providence?

Marcia said she often wondered if she might become an alcoholic, "but I saw your suffering and when I see some of my friends drink too much, all I think of is suffering."

From Paul, Jr.: "I never had the desire to drink anything more than a beer now and then. Whether your drinking had an influence or not, I don't know. But I know that it's not because a little buzzer goes on in my head to warn me. I just never cared for it. When I was in high school I had two marijuana cigarettes, and that was it. I found it boring. None of that stuff's ever been a problem with me, and I don't know the reason."

And from Georgia: "The very first drink I ever had was when I was in my sophomore year at college, even though I saw my friends drinking when we were in high school. Once since then I had too much to drink at a party and I almost dozed off at the wheel of my car. Brother, that was it. It always seemed like a whole lot of trouble to me."

The remark by Paul, Jr., that my drinking wasn't "that big a deal" for him resembles that of Dick Van Dyke's nineteen-year-old daughter. "When I asked her about my drinking later," Van Dyke revealed, "she said she didn't know anything about it. My kids knew I drank too much, and that my wife drank too much, but it was a solitary thing we did together. So I think my kids thought probably everybody did that and didn't realize we were alcoholic. But I'm sure there was a lot of lost time I could have spent with the kids."

Joy Baker, the recovered alcoholic wife of Senator Howard Baker, had lesser luck with her children. She related how her son, Darek, disposed of bottles she had cached, a maneuver that made her "furious," and quoted her daughter, Cindy: "I don't know how dad did it. He never broke down. He never gave up. I did. I said, 'Let her go, she'll never get well.' At one point I turned on him for not giving up. He told me she'd pull through it some day and be all right. When she decided to stop drinking, it threw us all off balance."

Some recognized experts on the problem, like Vernon Johnson, are convinced that the only difference between the alcoholic and his nonalcoholic loved ones is that one is physically affected by the chemical; otherwise, all have all the other symptoms. The "dry" are as sick as the drunk, except that the bodily damage is not there. With every drunk there is a sick "dry" who is almost a mirror image.

Carry Amelia Nation, the hatchet-swinging, saloon-smashing temperance advocate, divorced her first husband, who was an alcoholic. Because he was an active member of a fraternal order, she later turned her fury against such organizations, then against tobacco, foreign foods, corsets, skirts that were not long enough for her liking and paintings of nudes. Her second husband, David Nation, divorced her on grounds of desertion. The Encyclopaedia Britannica called her autobiography "a hodgepodge of disorder." She had such a morbid preoccupation with liquor that she couldn't hang on to her husbands and all but neglected her daughter.

I have to believe that Carry Nation, who would never let a drop sully her lips, had a monumental booze problem. Alcoholism is, indeed, a "family disease."

SIXTEEN

Suddenly it was New Year's Eve 1967, and it was incredible that time had raced by so swiftly while I was bent over the typewriter.

Time had raced by for everyone else, too, but it hit me with a special impact because suddenly my column was ten years old. Where had the years gone?

When the late publisher Marshall Field IV brought me to the Chicago *Sun-Times*, he placed me under contract to write a television column. I had just ended three years of writing such a column for the Scripps-Howard chain. I suggested that television as it was then (1957), and as I felt it would become later, did not have the force to sustain reader interest on a daily basis in a column of personal opinion. Certainly programing itself and show business goings-on should be covered as news items, but I argued that as a columnist I would need a wider range of subject matter. Field agreed, but the unwritten arrangement was that I would write the column for five years and then move on to other things.

I don't know what happened when the five years were up—obviously we all forgot about it—but the column was successful (of the twenty-five major features in the paper, it was consistently in the top three), and now it was ten years old and time I did something else.

But I didn't. Newspapers are notorious for being slow and reluctant to change, and I continued to write the column for another six years. One day in 1972 I decided I was written out. I had said all I had to say and now I was not only repeating myself, I was interviewing myself. After nineteen years of daily column pressure—during which I had written the equivalent of fifty-seven fat books (by word count)—I told my editor the column needed a new, fresh approach, and so did I. I had hoped to move to the editorial page, but I was appointed writer of special features, specializing in personality profiles and series.

Three years later, in mid-January 1975, my wife filed for separate maintenance. On February 14, a week after winning the United Press International Award for feature writing, I walked into the office of J. G. Trezevant, executive vice-president of Field Enterprises, Inc., and Field's right-hand man, and turned in my signed resignation. Incidentally, Trezevant and Robert W. McAllister, Field's vice-president for industrial relations, were extremely generous in the financial arrangements of my departure. I could not have asked for better treatment.

Now I was about to begin the great adventure of free-lance writing. No more daily deadlines. No more rushing to the train in the morning and rushing to the train at night. I would be living alone, so I would have solitude to write. It was beatific."

But it was also a double trauma. After thirty-four years as a newspaperman, I found myself without a newspaper. After thirty years of marriage to the same woman, I was alone. After the cacophony, the ecstatic whoop-and-holler hindrance of eight children, there was only silence.

And there was the sinister shadow of alcoholism. It would not—it would never—go away.

Naturally there had been a vast amount of drinking during the years of the column, and while this in no sense excuses my attraction to the gargle, my exposure to it was uncommonly frequent. Whenever I started my day by interviewing an actress at ten o'clock in the morning in her hotel suite, where her agents had set up a bar, and the choice was between bloody marys and coffee, I almost invariably chose bloody marys—at ten o'clock in the morning. Not unusually, the rest of the day might include lunch (with drinks) with some director or producer, a cocktail party or reception and, fairly often, an end-of-the-day interview or dinner where liquor flowed. For three years I kept a diary of my daily activities (I had the vague notion that I might someday write a book about it), and as I reread it I was jolted by the number of functions I had to attend every day where drinking was routine. Certainly, at no time did anyone pin me down and pour the tiger milk down my throat; I did it all by myself. But it was there, constantly.

Especially hazardous were my trips to Hollywood and New York, particularly Hollywood. When a columnist involved with show business hits Hollywood, every agent in town knows it and the glad hands are almost suffocating. It was fairly standard to walk into my hotel room and find seven or eight bottles of liquor, each with a card from some network, studio or agent welcoming me to town, promising to call and insisting "Let me know if there's anything I can do for you." More often than not there would even be a courtesy bottle from the hotel manager.

Once I complained to my editor—my first editor on the *Sun-Times*—that there were too many affairs to attend and could someone else be assigned to share them. "Nonsense," he said, "the paper has to be represented and you've got to be at those things." He even told me I wasn't visiting Hollywood and New York often enough. I am not shifting blame to the paper's editorship; it was simply that they were not aware then that I was an alcoholic (I wasn't aware), and that this much exposure to drink was a high risk. Oddly enough, I drank little on these trips. I'm not sure why; perhaps it was my instinctive belief that I represented a distinguished newspaper and it was imperative that I behave. I do know that I was nervous about drinking on the road, but felt safe about it when I was home. (Looking back, perhaps that was the reason I wanted to move to the safety of the editorial page.)

It was after I dropped the column and became a feature writer that I noticed a change in my drinking pattern. Now the morning drink started, and for the first time I found it necessary to leave my desk and go out for a couple of drams. Toward the end I was having a drink or two before reaching the office and would slip away on occasion during the day for relief.

During the next four years, after my resignation, I lived in nine different places—all of them within a half hour of the children—and in that time I learned, painfully, that the greatest threat to sobriety was living alone. After reading the documents that said my marriage had ended (that was never going to happen to *me!*), I found lodgings in a non-denominational Christian retreat house. In the time I was there—I was in touch with dozens of people, most of them of a religious bent—I had almost no interest in drinking. I think I might have remained there longer than five months were it not for a paunchy, early-fortyish Protestant minister who kept nettling me with requests to find him female companionship.

"Come now," he would say, "surely a man in your position has got to know a lot of women in Chicago. Why don't you put me in touch with some of them?"

One Sunday, after attending an evening worship service,

he accosted me on the way out of the chapel. Still clad in his clerical robe, he again pleaded that I get him a woman.

Perhaps it was his poor timing—he had just delivered a sermon—but his behavior vexed me so much that I said, "Doesn't it bother you, Reverend, to keep asking me something like that?"

"Why," he replied, "don't you think I want to get laid like anybody else?"

I am not a prude, but the idea of practically pimping for a man of the cloth was repugnant, and I left. I took a small furnished apartment and was drinking within two days. After a period of hospitalization I decided that I was not yet ready for the bachelor life and moved into a halfway house, where I had ten months of total sobriety. Perhaps the discipline was a factor. Most of the residents were alcoholics, and some were ex-convicts using alcoholic rehabilitation as a means for parole. We paid what we could afford, but we were given various chores. I became an expert dishwasher and a passable sandwich maker, but for most of my stay there my assignment was mopping floors and keeping the bathrooms clean. It was a sterling, if austere, exercise in humility.

I learned other things. I learned that an alcoholic can experience a seizure months after he has sobered up. I spent most of one memorable night keeping such a victim from swallowing his tongue before medical help arrived. I also learned that a sobered-up alcoholic can suffer delirium tremens as long as a year after taking his last drink, that in 25 percent of the cases the DTs are fatal, and if you survive two attacks you should be ready to travel, because on the third one you are likely to be leaving for that Big Barroom in the Sky.

After ten months of communal, sober life, I convinced

myself I was ready to venture into the real world again. I left, got drunk, found a furnished apartment, bought three hundred dollars' worth of pots, pans, dishes, groceries, and so forth, and moved in. The morning after the first night in my new diggings, I awoke to find that the bathroom had a shower but no tub. Obviously, I had returned to drinking with a vengeance, because the lack of a tub was something I hadn't noticed while inspecting the apartment. After a few morning drinks, I decided I could not live in a tubless flat. Explaining this to the dismayed landlady was so embarrassing, and I felt so bad about having put her out, that I made her a gift of everything I'd bought (she had a month's rent in advance) and set out to find another apartment. This is classic alcoholic behavior.

So, on to another apartment—and another drinking disaster.

From there I moved to yet another nondenominational retreat house for a second interlude of community living. I was there six months and, again, seemingly under the influence of people around me, I never gave drinking a thought. In addition, I stopped smoking for half a year (probably because smoking was not permitted in the house). This, however, was a charismatic, laying-on-of-hands type of establishment and I had the misfortune to be espoused by a self-ordained revivalist who made it his mission to make me born-again against my will. He was, oddly enough, a Jew who had converted to Christianity and who, while speaking in tongues, insisted on periodically anointing my forehead with Wesson oil, which he kept in the refrigerator. He could not understand why I preferred attending AA meetings to participating in the hand-clapping, hymn-singing sessions over which he presided at night. The more I resisted, the angrier he became, until finally he scolded:

"You're sinning in the face of the Lord Jesus Christ when you go to AA meetings!"

"Whatever do you mean?" I said. "I go there because I want to be a better man."

"It's in the Bible!" he shouted. "You're insulting Jesus Christ by turning to other men, drunken sinners like you, instead of turning to Jesus Christ. You're showing you have no faith by seeking the help of mere men instead of divine help. It's in the Bible. Everything's in the Bible! The Bible is all you need to stop drinking!"

The standoff came to an acrid climax one night when he sermonized the residents, "We have among us one who is really not with us, one who rejects the divine healing of Jesus Christ through our hands by asking for help from other sinners instead of allowing us to heal him through Jesus Christ. This man is a Satan in disguise who has come here to destroy this blessed house!"

I had not come to the house for any religious reason. I did not want to be saved. I had come there for a solitude I believed possible among spiritually inclined people and which I felt I needed, since I seemed to be drinking only when alone. But after the "Satan" insinuation I decided to leave. In fact, I departed in fear because I truly felt this man was a fanatic. Besides, I didn't like the smell of Wesson oil on my face.

Another apartment, another drinking disaster and another period of hospitalization.

From there I took myself to an alcoholism treatment center—not as a patient but as an unpaid employee. In return for bed and board I directed its public relations and even filled in as a substitute counselor whenever a staff member was absent. After thirteen months of complete sobriety, I wearied of group life and longed for the outside world and life as a normal individual.

Another apartment, another drinking disaster and yet another hospitalization.

This time I came close to tying my previous record (two days) for shortness of time spent in an apartment. This one was in a private home owned by a divorcee in her fifties, the mother of a grown son and daughter, who lived with her. On my second day there, she came into my quarters with a bottle of whisky, two glasses and some ice. Her children were away for the weekend and I noticed that she had already been drinking (at noon). I also noticed that she was in her nightgown, had on a robe and was barefoot. It was uncanny, like something in a bad movie. Within a minute or so she had poured two drinks and had her bare feet atop my desk, giving me an uncomfortable view of her nightgown. I was curious, and since she had dispensed with preliminaries, I decided to do likewise.

"Do you always drink at noon?" I asked.

"No."

"What made you bring a bottle in here?"

"I don't know. I heard you typing all night and I thought you could use a drink."

I excused myself. "I don't drink whisky," I said. "I'll go get a bottle of vodka."

I stayed away two days drinking vodka, which a Russian proverb describes as "the aunt of wine." When I returned, she didn't ask where I had been, but she had obviously understood that I preferred the company of my aunt to hers. That night I packed my cartons again and left the next day, going back to the Drake Oak Brook Hotel again to do some thinking—and drinking.

I called Dr. Charles Anderson in Hinsdale, who again came to my rescue. It may be true that doctors no longer make house calls, but I was lucky enough to have the friendship of a psychiatrist who did. He recommended that

I check into the Alcoholism Rehabilitation Service of the Hinsdale San. I did, and it was one of the most beneficial decisions I had ever made, because I learned more about myself and my drinking in the Hinsdale San program than I had in all of the other treatment centers and hospitals put together. I have to say flatly that for me, an experienced alcoholic, the Hinsdale San's program was superior to anything I had encountered.

During the years of wandering from place to place, from community living to aloneness, I tried to settle down and return to serious writing. But it was a start-and-stop scenario. While I had done some drinking at work during my last two years with the paper, I had barely done any drinking on the job during the years of the column or when I was writing books. I had often thought of it, mindful of author E. B. White, who had said, "Before I start to write, I always treat myself to a nice dry martini. Just one, to get started. After that, I'm on my own."

Despite all that I had learned in AA and in rehab programs, I still felt that somehow I could emerge as a social drinker. Perhaps now, writing without the pressure of newspaper deadlines, I could have a drink—just one, like White—to "get started." But for me one drink was too many and twenty were not enough.

I did manage to get halfway through a book, but one night, while in a post-drinking depression, I read it over and decided it was not worthy of me. I tore it up and threw it into the garbage. I was being grandiose and dramatic. "I'll start fresh tomorrow," I told myself. Of course I did not. Later I did get down about thirty thousand words of a novel I owed my publisher (which I did not throw away), but I set it aside as a change began to take hold of my personality.

I sensed that creatively I was next to worthless when I was alone, but I was able to assume my responsibilities when I was with others. Yet I found myself wanting to be alone more and more, even though there was no remedy for the pain that aloneness brought. I sought relief in liquor, of course—the "anesthetic" my daughter Nelda recalled—but there was never any relief. The suffering only got worse.

Eventually I felt that I was being masochistic about it. I was steadfast in my desire to live within the immediate area of my children because I loved them too much to put a great distance between us. Yet I kept my distance. When they invited me to dinner or to other functions, I made up excuses and declined. I wanted to be with them, yet even when I was not drinking I would turn down most of their requests for get-togethers. Then I would sit in front of the typewriter and wonder why I had done such a thing, because I loved and needed them. I already knew that then. What I did not realize was that they loved and needed *me*. But I theorized that pity and perhaps a little guilt were what motivated their desire to be with me. I did not give a thought to love. And I did not want to be pitied; shame now had me in a stranglehold.

And through it all ran the anguish and torment of loneliness, which, I now feel, embodies all of the suffering of all the imaginable ailments put together. If there is one ache that could possibly describe the worst that can befall a human being, I think it would be the wrenching pain of loneliness. I remember frequently longing for the cries and the laughter of our noisy household. I would bang cupboard doors to break the intolerable silence and stomp away from the typewriter, moaning, "Where did everybody go?"

The years after the separation were a round of reading, writing, drinking and playing Scrabble (another addiction) with my AA sponsor, Jim. The wall I had erected around myself was rising higher.

Gradually I began to think of the drinking insanity that had affected writers—Edgar Allan Poe ("What disease is like alcohol!" cries the narrator in the story "The Black Cat"); F. Scott Fitzgerald; William Faulkner; Ring Lardner; Ernest Hemingway, and so many others. And I thought of the madness that attended the drinking of such writers as Jack London and Eugene O'Neill.

London maintained he was not an alcoholic, though he wrote toward the end of his life, "I have achieved a condition in which my body was never free from alcohol. Nor did I permit myself to be away from alcohol. I was carrying a beautiful alcoholic conflagration around with me. There was no time, in my waking time, that I didn't want a drink."

According to my reading of London's life, deep down he had admitted to himself that he was an alcoholic, but he was unable to accept it. I considered his outward denial and his refusal to accept the illness, and wondered if this might someday be true of me. Or was it already? Certainly I was flirting with insanity. I don't mean the insanity of things done under the influence, which were beyond the control of the mind, but the insanity of thoughts *prior* to drinking. For how could a man in his right mind, knowing the pain and guilt and remorse that follow prolonged drinking, deliberately and soberly set out to drink again? This was the hint of insanity I feared.

There was more, and it centered on guilt which had its roots in early childhood. I had been educated solely by nuns and Jesuits, and in the area of morality the only sins I learned of were those of impurity and drunkenness (it was called inebriation in those days). I can't recall that there were other immoral things going on in the world, but I do remember having it hammered into us that adulterers and inebriates were the ones condemned to the eternal flames of hell.

Adding to this hangup was a precept that my father, an eloquent man, had voiced when I was about fourteen. I cannot recall his exact words, but it went something like this:

"Never forget that the worst day a man will ever face will be the day he stands at the Last Judgment, and his God asks him, 'What did you do with the gifts I gave you?' We all will have to answer that awful question."

He went on to explain about the blind and the deaf and the other disabled and handicapped who would stand next to us, "perhaps with envy in their eyes. All of us," he continued, "will one day have to account for the time and the gifts we received. For some of us, it will be the moment of terror."

That stayed with me through the years. Because of my drinking, it was not a terror that would come after I died, but a terror that was with me each time I drank.

Together with the loneliness that never went away, it was agony. And agony is the struggle before death.

SEVENTEEN

For John Brennan it was the classic American success story. In his thirty-one years with the Ford Motor Company he had risen from tightening bolts on the assembly line to board chairman and managing director of Ford of Switzerland. During his climb up the corporate ladder he became an alcoholic. Now he was suing Ford for $1.3 million, claiming that the job turned him into a drunk and forced him into early retirement.

As explained in his suit, Brennan began drinking seriously in 1950, while representing Ford in Washington, D.C., where his superiors complimented him on his ability to hold his drink. Later he served as a liaison officer for Ford at the United Nations, where his drinking increased at the delegates' bar. He was promoted to higher posts in the Netherlands and Austria, where he began drinking alone, and finally to the top-salaried job in Switzerland. "At no time was I offered help of any kind," he claimed, and when he sought help the company asked him to resign. His marriage broke up, he underwent treatment, recovered, and is now financial administrator for a treatment center in Michigan. (Ford had an overseas treatment center for its U.S. employees, but Brennan maintained that while he was abroad he was never told that such help was available.) In June 1979 Brennan told me he had withdrawn the suit for personal reasons.

In 1970 Patrolman John Cursey of the Memphis Police Department shot and killed two holdup men during a liquor store robbery. A week after the killings his friends presented him with a fifth of whisky. Over the label they pasted a police photo of one of the dead bandits sprawled on the floor of the liquor store. Six months later Cursey was an alcoholic.

He said—and psychiatrists backed him—that he relived the killings in his dreams and suffered severe anxiety and depressive neuroses. His wife left him. In 1976 he was fired for "uncontrollable" drinking. Two years later the Memphis Pension Board awarded him a disability of five thousand dollars a year—the first it had ever granted for psychological injuries.

These incidents dramatize the increasing, but insufficient, involvement of employers in the alcoholism of employees. Alcoholism is called the "$15-billion hangover" because that is the annual cost to U.S. industry of problem workers, from executives to laborers, who lose an average of twenty-two working days a year.

A special report to Congress by the National Institute on Alcohol Abuse and Alcoholism, prepared in 1977 with the help of the Harvard School of Public Health, revealed that alcoholism costs ten billion dollars a year in absenteeism, medical expenses and poor job performance, another three billion in property damage, workmen's compensation and insurance, and two billion in health and welfare costs.

Alcoholism is referred to as the disease of denial, and in industry denial is also a symptom of the employer. Much of industry still looks at the disease as unmentionable and untreatable. Until very recently a businessman might say, "We don't have any problems with alcoholics; we fire

them." Or if an employer discovered a drinking problem
among his employees, the tendency might be to cover up
for them. This is dangerous since the NIAAA estimates
that 5 percent of the nation's work force—white and blue
collar—are alcoholics, and another 5 percent are problem
drinkers (and potential alcoholics).

But in the dual-denial syndrome, industry has the advantage. Studies conducted over a period of years show that industry has the most effective motivational tool known
today for helping the alcoholic overcome his problem: his
desire to keep his job. Often this is more important to the
employee than is his family or his health. Unfortunately,
according to the *Journal of American Insurance*, of the
million and a half companies in the United States, only
fifteen hundred have instituted any alcoholism control programs, despite such warnings as the following, by Dr. Sel-
don Bacon of the Rutgers Center of Alcohol Studies:
"When you have a hidden problem drinker who signs contracts or makes investments, he can lose $1 million in five
minutes."

Companies that complain they can't afford such programs are told by those who have studied the problem that
they can. After all, it is cheaper and easier to retain and re-
habilitate alcoholics than it is to fire them and rehire and
train replacements who may end up having the same
problem.

Raymond J. Kelly, former industrial coordinator of employee alcoholism programs for the Illinois Department of
Mental Health, said that giving the alcoholic the option of
treatment or risking dismissal usually leads him to the company program, which has two superior features: a policy
statement from the company which gives the employee the
same consideration as any other sick worker (his job secu-
rity will not be jeopardized if he accepts the program), and

assurance that job performance will be the only basis for his company's concern (the boss is not looking for alcoholics but for employees who are not working up to par).

Kelly, now administrator of employee alcoholism programs for the Sears Roebuck Company in Chicago, has stated, "The policy statement should have further assurance that medical records of alcoholic employees will be kept confidential, and that the employer will collaborate with the union if there is one."

Insurance coverage for alcoholism programs should not be a problem. Normally, if alcoholism is not excluded from the company's health policy, treatment is covered (as it is with Blue Cross, Blue Shield, Medicare and Medicaid). According to Kelly, "The most expensive way to handle problem workers is to fire or ignore them, the most profitable way is to help them recover. Sixty to eighty per cent of those referred for help achieve rehabilitation and once again become productive persons."

It was in order to once again become a productive person that I made the call to Dr. Anderson, which led to my going into the Hinsdale San's rehabilitation program. I was too embarrassed by repeated relapses to even tell Jim, my AA sponsor, that I was doing so. But prior to checking into the Hinsdale San I found solace in something Dr. Morris Chafetz had written:

"A colleague once remarked that people were disappointed in the psychiatric treatment of depression. They thought that the treated person would never get depressed again. That's a pretty unrealistic expectation in view of the state of the world. People have the same kinds of expectations for the alcoholic's recovery. He's not allowed any relapses or slips. But who goes through life without setbacks? And when we do experience setbacks, it's quite common for us to return to patterns of coping that are familiar or have brought us relief in the past. I am not surprised that a person with a long history of problems with alcohol regresses to the relief of alcoholic anesthesia in the face of some overwhelming stress and pain. But our demands are so high, and we make alcoholics feel so guilty and lost if they slip, that the slip often turns into a complete relapse.

"Instead of celebrating whatever period of self-respect, dignity and functioning the alcoholic person enjoys, we signal our feeling of pessimism about his or her recovery. We wait—as we force the person to do—with bated breath for a relapse. Then our prophecy is fulfilled. A rheumatologist thinks he's doing very well if his arthritic patient is pain-free and functioning for six months or longer. Other specialists, too, are grateful for [a] less than perfect, permanent cure. Those treating alcoholics should offer a realistic helping hand, aiming for [a] cure but happy with good periods of recovery."

According to the American Medical Association, "In treatment, abstinence is sought as a primary objective. But additional considerations, such as improved social or occupational adjustments, may be far better guides in evaluating the success or failure of a treatment effort. Temporary relapse with return to drinking, then, should not be equated with failure, any more than should the diabetic's occasional discontinuation of his diet or insulin."

I ran into a stern, occasionally patronizing reaction to relapse in, of all places, AA. As in most organizations, there is in AA a sort of fellowship of elder statesmen comprising members who joined and never touched a drop for ten, fifteen or twenty years or more. It is customary that a member who has fallen off the wagon admit this to his peers when he returns to a meeting. On occasion I would hear veiled admonitions from some of the elder statesmen claiming that I was something less than a good influence on the group. Of course, the vast majority of AA members adhered to the parable of the prodigal son and warmly welcomed the returnee back to the fold. I shall always remember the comment a member made when this theme was under discussion. Gazing knowingly at some old-timers who had been sober many years, he said, "We take this thing one day at a time only. The soberest person in this room tonight is the one who got up the earliest this morning."

The fact that my picture topped my newspaper column every day for so many years made me well known in the Chicago area, and I soon learned I was not to enjoy the anonymity I had expected. Shortly after joining AA, I began receiving calls from strangers, who would say, "Welcome to the club, pal; I'm glad you made it." This was meant to be complimentary, and I appreciated the compassion, but I could not help wondering why word should get around so quickly that I was an alcoholic and why they were talking about me among themselves.

I frequented many AA groups and it was not unusual, on arrival at a meeting, to run into someone who knew me who would proceed to introduce me to his friends with the remark, "This is Paul Molloy. You've read his stuff," or, after my comment at a meeting, to hear another member say, "It was good to hear that comment from Paul. He's a writer and I wish I had his way with words." Once, in a hospital where I was a patient, we started a session before a large group (including nonalcoholic outsiders) by introducing ourselves by our first names. After I'd said, "I'm Paul, and I'm an alcoholic," a man at the other end of the room literally sprang from his chair, pointed to me and said: "Hey, you're Paul Molloy, the columnist!" On another occasion an AA member asked me to be his guest at a Sunday breakfast meeting of his neighborhood group. He had the gall to ask me to ask two alcoholic friends of mine, a man prominent in Major League baseball and a well-known television personality, to attend with me. He was blatantly out to make an impression, and I declined, a bit firmly, by asking him whatever had happened to anonymity.

What rankled a lot was being told by some AA members that the reason for my relapses was that I did not go to more meetings. Often I was told that I should go to a meeting every night and during the day as well. These people meant well, but they did not seem to understand that my way of life did not make it possible for me to make AA all of my life. Some of them were in their sixties and had retired; I had eight children to raise and a column to write every day. It soon became evident that others attended meetings each night because it was a means of getting away from their wives or husbands, or because they had made AA the core of their social lives. Their stresses and strains were not my stresses and strains. Besides, I had not yet fully surrendered; they were fortunate in that they had.

Dr. Chafetz has commented on this point: "Remarkable as AA is, it's not for everyone. There are those of us who are private people and abhor the exposure that AA requires. Others have other needs. AA has not been willing in the past (it is improving) to understand that some people need more than just AA, or not even AA. The pressures are now immense to join if you are alcoholic—recovered or not.

"I recently heard of a well-known person who had recovered from alcoholism without AA. He had been making a name for himself in the alcoholism community but was not looked upon with complete favor because he had not made it through AA. Ten years after his recovery, he began to feel he wouldn't have all the credentials to be effective in the field unless he was a member of AA. So he joined."

Another observation by Dr. Chafetz also made an impression on me. Discussing whether alcoholics are always alcoholics, he said, "Most recovered alcoholics say they are. They say it with pride for having recovered and as a reminder that they think alcohol is still a danger to them. I suspect that there's nothing wrong with their position. My concern is that an illness not become the identity of a person. I'm uncomfortable when a person is called a diabetic or a cardiac. People are dehumanized when they're labeled by a condition."

The occasional discomfiture I found in AA sounds like criticism; it is something more than that. I send it up as a sort of storm signal for those who will be joining the movement. There will be disappointments and letdowns, but then one finds these in any project one joins, be it a church, a country club, a fraternity or a bowling team. All of us, in and out of AA, are individuals with different moods, personalities and attitudes; our reactions are dissimilar, and some of us are more sensitive than others (I know I was too sensitive). Yet if Dr. Chafetz was right when he said that AA is not for everyone, I know it was for me. I never turned my back on it; I dropped out now and then, but I always returned as quickly as I could and was grateful to do so because it was responsible for my finding the patchwork on-again-off-again sobriety I did get, and it may be responsible for the permanent sobriety I hope to achieve if ever I come to terms with total surrender. I am on record as owing my life to Dr. Anderson (and the Seventh-Day Adventist people at the Hinsdale San), but one of the first things Dr. Anderson did was send me a pair of Good Samaritans from AA. That is where it all began, and I shall always treasure that.

Something else I shall always treasure—and have read a hundred times or more—is an article written some time ago by Fulton Oursler. His alcoholic relative's recovery inspired the author of *The Greatest Story Ever Told* to write in a now-defunct magazine:

"Down at the very bottom of the social scale of AA society are the pariahs, the untouchables, the outcasts, all underprivileged and all known by one terrible epithet—relatives. I am a relative. I know my place. I am not complaining. But I hope no one will mind if I venture the plaintive confession that there are times, oh, so many times, when I wish I had been an alcoholic. The reason is that I consider the AA people the most charming in the world.

"Such is my considered opinion. As a journalist it has been my fortune to meet many of the people who are considered charming. I number among my friends stars and lesser lights of stage and screen. Writers are my daily diet. I know the ladies and gentlemen of both political parties. I have been entertained in the White House. I have broken bread with kings and ministers and ambassadors. And I say, after that catalog, that I would prefer an evening with my AA friends to any person or group of persons I have indicated.

"I asked myself why I consider so charming these alcoholic caterpillars who have found their butterfly wings in AA. I can name a few reasons. The AA people are what they are, and they were what they were, because they are sensitive, imaginative, possessed of a sense of humor and an awareness of universal truth.

"They are sensitive, which means they hurt easily, and that helped them become alcoholics. But when they have found their restoration, they are still as sensitive as ever—

responsive to beauty and truth, and eager about the intangible glories of this life. That makes them charming companions. And they are possessed of a sense of universal truth that is often a new thing in their hearts. The fact that this at-one feeling with God's universe had never been awakened in them is sometimes the reason why they drank.

"The fact that it was at last awakened is almost always the reason why they were restored to the good and simple ways of life. Stand with them when the meeting is over, and listen as they say the 'Our Father.'

"They have found a power greater than themselves which they serve diligently. And that gives them a charm that never was elsewhere on land and sea. It makes you know that God Himself is really charming, because the AA people reflect His mercy and His forgiveness.

"They are imaginative, and that helped to make them alcoholics. Some of them drank to flog their imaginations on to greater things. Others guzzled only to black out unendurable visions that rose in their imaginations. But when they have found their restoration, their imagination is responsive to new thinking, and their talk abounds with color and light. And that, too, makes them charming companions.

"They are possessed of a sense of humor. Even in their cups they have been known to say damnably funny things. Often, it was being forced to take seriously the little and mean things of life that made them seek escape in the bottle. But when they have found their restoration, their sense of humor finds a blessed freedom, and they are able to reach a god-like state, where they can laugh at themselves— the very height of self-conquest. Go to meetings, and listen to their laughter. What are they laughing at? At ghoulish memories over which weaker souls would cringe in useless remorse. And that makes them wonderful people to be with by candle-light.

"AA can, and does, show these people a solution to their problem, and its greatest recommendation is—it works!"

EIGHTEEN

•

A day or two after I started the Hinsdale San's four-week
rehab project, I told the counselors that three weeks into
the program I would have to take a night off to fulfill a
speaking engagement. They were not too pleased with the
idea of my leaving the unit, even for a few hours. Passes
were against the rules, but since I had committed myself to
the speech months earlier, there was no way to cancel out.

On the night of my talk before a women writers' group
thirty miles from the hospital, there appeared, courtesy of
the counselors, a combination chauffeur-chaperon. He was
a recovering alcoholic who had recently "graduated" from
the program, and he had instructions to drive me to the library, sit in on my spiel, and deliver me back to the hospital sober. I was a bit miffed to be assigned a guardian angel
for the venture, but since I had mentioned at a session that
I liked a drink before giving a lecture, I understood the
counselors' concern.

My shepherd was a genial fellow and a hit with the ladies, so I introduced him as a fellow writer. After the talk,
a couple of the women asked me what kind of writing he
had done. "He's written quite a bit of fiction," I said airily.
It was not entirely a lie; during his drinking career my
friend had written a startling number of bad checks.

I mention the incident to illustrate the rigidity and discipline of the Hinsdale San's treatment program. It is based on one developed by Vernon E. Johnson, of the Johnson Alcoholism Institute, for several hospitals. At one of them, St. Mary's Hospital in Minneapolis, annual studies show that 52 percent of the patients do not drink again after completing the program. The other 48 percent relapse and experiment with alcohol. About half of these dropouts return and complete the two-year after-care program and remain abstinent. This translates as three out of four recoveries. Doctors alone cannot achieve this score because alcoholism is not just an ailment of the body. Since it's more than an emotional affliction, psychiatrists alone cannot do it. And since it's not solely a spiritual problem, clergymen or religion are not sufficient. Whole treatment, therefore, must consider the mental, physical, social and spiritual aspects of the individual, with a view to bringing the patient back to reality. Sobriety is not just a matter of putting the cork on the bottle; since the disease involves the victim physically, psychologically, and spiritually, it is a matter of changing the thinking and attitudes—restoration of adequate ego strength to enable the alcoholic to once again cope with life situations. If the whole man is not treated simultaneously, according to Johnson, relapse is inevitable:

"If the emotional disorder alone is reduced, the patient leaves medical care thinking he can 'handle it' now that he feels well. Then his experimentation with alcohol wipes out the gains made in his emotional environment and sends him plunging down the same old self-destructive spiral. Or if only the mental mismanagement is brought under control (awareness and acceptance of the logical reasons for abstinence), the emotional burdens continue in force. The patient remains easily irritated, anxious, nervous or depressed. The mass of free-floating negative feelings is still present, bringing on waves of self-pity and resentment.

He overacts to simple frustrations; he is judgemental, omnipotent, hypersensitive, tense and unpredictable. In fact, his family reports, he was easier to live with when he was drinking. The symptoms of the 'dry drunk' are most evident and damaging to family and others immediately around the sick person. Both of these conditions, mental and emotional, must be reduced if he is to be stabilized into a chemically-free life style."

During my four weeks in the Hinsdale San's program, I attended almost sixty lectures, saw eight films and was firmly directed to four AA meetings a week. One of the activities I came to appreciate was one to which I was at first hostile. This activity involved a confrontation between the patient and members of his family, before the other patients, during which his family told it like it was. In my case, my daughters, Lisa and Marcia, armed with notes, told me what it was like for them when I was drinking. Before these sessions the "interveners" are told that the "evidence" they've gathered must be about specific incidents and must be presented before the whole group in a non-judgmental fashion. The reason for this session, painful as it is, is sound: As the alcoholic moves into his bizarre behavior, many around him tend to keep it to themselves because of misplaced loyalty to the sick person. This supports the sickness, since they become "enablers" of the developing condition, permitting it, by their silence, to go to tragic lengths before any intervention occurs. I was not allowed to question my daughters while they gave their "evidence"; I had to remain silent, but I flinched a lot. It was only after a later session, where the group questioned me about my daughters' data, that it sank in that I had been told, in a *receivable fashion*, the things I had either forgotten or ignored. I realized that my children cared enough to risk describing my life to me in ways I did not know, to bring me back to reality.

In the spring of 1979 a "drinkathon" for charity made the front pages of the Chicago newspapers (and probably elsewhere). It consisted of a sponsored tour of the thirty-three bars on one street in Peoria, Illinois, by a group of people eager to help the Peoria Association for Retarded Children. The fund-raisers went on an all-day, six-and-a-half-mile bar-hopping trek, spurred by sponsors who had pledged a certain amount of money for each tavern visited. The story was accompanied by a picture of a participant who had passed out beside his car. A few days later the Chicago *Tribune* editorialized, "The 'drinkathon' deserves the booby prize as the worst charitable promotion of the decade. Our report of this bizarre event was illustrated by a picture captioned, 'After tying one on for charity, a man falls out for a nap'—beside his car. Of course, 'drinkathon' participants could not be expected to walk between thirty-three bars along the route. The take of the Peoria 'drink-athon' was about $1,500. A single drunk driving accident could cost far more than that. There is a proposal before the Illinois General Assembly to put a tax on liquor to help defray some of the public health costs that can be traced to it. That may be a somewhat farout idea, but it is in a more sound direction than are 'drinkathons' for charity."

The "charity" event in Peoria makes it evident that more education is needed in the area of alcohol abuse. A step in that direction was taken in May 1979 when the Senate voted to require a health-warning label on all bottles of liquor, similar to the one on cigarette packages. The label, which would be affixed to bottles containing more than 24 percent alcohol, would read, "Consumption of al-

coholic beverages may be hazardous to your health." I do
not think the label would greatly deter adult imbibers, just
as I do not think the warning on cigarettes has caused a
great many adults to quit smoking. But I think that the
warning on cigarettes has some effect on youngsters just beginning to smoke or who are tempted. Similarly, I think a
label on bottles would carry a disturbing message for young
people just starting to drink.

I wish such warnings had been around when I had my
first flirtations with booze. (At that time we couldn't spell
the word "cirrhosis," let alone know what it meant.) If I
was born to be what I am, an "instant alcoholic," labels
probably would not have changed the course of my life.
But I have the notion that they would have stopped me
short, now and then, and made me think about the danger
of abusing my body and brain. If nothing else, the warnings, along with more effective means of education, would
have made the drinking uncomfortable. I wish now that
the hazards of overindulgence had been taught to me in
school—there was little cause for it to come up at home.
Instead I was inculcated with the awesome fear that
drinking was one of the two immoralities that would send
me to hell for eternity. Instead of turning me away from
the bottle, this sort of tactic only made me feel guilty, and
as the years passed and my guilt increased, I found that an
effective way to disperse it was to drink more. It was a vicious, bibulous circle.

Certainly, a problem that affects seventy-five million
people and costs the nation's industry alone fifteen billion
dollars a year demands more attention from the government and the community. One can imagine the national
panic were Washington to suddenly announce that seventy-five million people lived under the threat of cholera;

it is quite likely that a national emergency would be declared. Yet alcoholism can be as deadly as cholera.

Certainly, a problem that is fastening its tentacles around the nation's teenagers deserves more attention than it is getting in primary and high schools. More children are drinking nowadays, and they are starting younger and drinking more often. According to a 1979 NIAAA report, the average age at which children take their first drink is eleven, and an estimated 40 percent have tasted alcohol by the age of ten. Since states began lowering the drinking age from twenty-one, arrests of young people for drunk driving have skyrocketed. The National Highway Traffic Safety Administration reported that in 1977 9 percent of all traffic fatalities involved drunken drivers under the age of twenty. The alcoholic tide has risen higher because of cheap, fast-selling "pop" wines which disguise their alcoholic content with fruit flavors. A spokesman for the Texas Council on Alcoholism complained, "Kids seem to look on the stuff as a zippy, sophisticated soft drink. But this 'kiddie stuff,' this pop wine, contains nine per cent alcohol—about twice as much as beer." The transition from soda pop to alcohol is made easy by these wines.

Education about drinking is plainly needed, starting in the lower grades, but a positive approach should be utilized, stressing the fact that alcohol is a friend to man and a pleasant social activity as long as it is not abused. Children should also be taught early that some people are prone to alcoholism, and that liquor therefore poses a threat to some drinkers, just as sugar poses a threat to the diabetic. At another level, newspapers, television and magazines waste entirely too much space and time on the freakish or funny aspects of alcoholism instead of helping to educate the public.

Of all the widely read, syndicated daily columnists with

whose writings I am familiar, Ann Landers, in my estimation, is the alcoholic's best friend. She has consistently counseled her readers who have an alcoholic problem (either the alcoholics themselves or their bewildered families) to get help as quickly as possible—to seek out AA, a clergyman-friend, a doctor, or all three. She is one columnist who is very much aware of the extensiveness and seriousness of the problem, and has practically become a crusader for the discouraged drinkers and their suffering loved ones.

Nor is the lack of education solely apparent in primary and high schools. Several doctors told me that in all their years as medical students and while interning, a grand total of one hour was devoted to alcoholism.

Meanwhile, there is something everyone can do about alcohol abuse: Take preventive measures to keep it from becoming a personal, fatal problem. If an individual suspects he has become dependent upon alcohol, he should lose no time in bringing his doubts to his family doctor (hopefully one who knows the subject). If he does not have a doctor in whom he can confide, he would do well to send for the "bible" of AA, a book called *Alcoholics Anonymous*, the "Big Book." It may be obtained by writing to Box 459, Grand Central Station, New York, New York 10017. Whomever the sufferer contacts, he should do it with total honesty, else the effort will be a waste of time and could make the situation worse. If treatment is called for, he should not hesitate to take it (chances are he is covered by some form of insurance). Submitting to the kind of treatment I have described could mean the difference between a life of serenity and a ride to either the madhouse or the cemetery.

During my month in the Hinsdale San's rehab program, I did more thinking about who I was and what I was than at any other period in my life. I had not come to grips with myself during other periods of hospitalization, and I don't know if the fault lay with their programs or with my stubbornness. I had had numerous confrontations with counselors, relatives and friends, but I had shunned the most important confrontation of all—the one with myself —probably because I knew what I would collide with and the prospect bothered me. Finally, I threw pride, grandiosity and ego aside and peered deeply and at length into my soul. What I saw there were three emotional upheavals that had crippled me during most of my life—guilt, discontent with myself and impatience—especially the last two, which I now know were intertwined.

It was in the days of college that I first noticed success did not go to my head; it simply flitted off somewhere, because I was never satisfied with it. It did not give me the elation I expected, and so it seemed to lack rewards. We would be near the end of a hockey game, well ahead and assured of winning, and my thoughts would be on the next game. Often, while boxing, I would find myself worrying about the match coming up next month instead of concentrating on the one at hand (a distraction which several times landed me on the canvas, knocked out).

One day, while working in the mines, I bought John Steinbeck's *The Grapes of Wrath*, became enchanted with it and told my brother, "Someday I'll have my name on a book like this." Twenty-two years later I did. The book was on the best-seller lists for three months, yet the rapture lasted little more than a week. Did I realize at that early date that I was not destined to be another Steinbeck? I tend to think so, else how could I explain the depression that followed? I went through the same malaise with succeeding books.

I had been a cub reporter in Montreal for about six months when, while walking with a colleague along St.

Catherine Street, I saw a newspaper truck carrying an advertisement which proclaimed, in big letters, "Read Walter Winchell Daily in the Montreal *Gazette*." I grabbed my friend's arm and said, half in jest, "Someday I'll have my name and my picture on a truck like that." Twenty years later it happened in Chicago. I remember being excited when I first saw it, but in a short time the thrill was gone. It is hard to explain the feeling, but it was as if I did not deserve it. I was not even able to accept congratulations; I was a little like the woman who, when complimented on her new hat or hairdo, replies, "Oh, it's just a little thing I picked up at a sale," or "I'm lucky, I have a terrific hairdresser." If an editor told me that a column or series I'd written was especially good, I'd say something like, "It wrote itself," or "it wasn't the writing—I had great subject matter."

I often wondered, during my years as newspaper reporter, magazine writer, columnist and author of books, why it was that I did not consider myself adequate in my career. Life had been good and I'd had more than average good luck. Still, the demon of discomposure hung on.

I now think it was related to guilt, because I was always conscious of the sacrifices my parents had made to give me a superior education. Simply stated, I felt guilty that Providence had been overly generous to me, but while I was drinking I was not living up to the expectations of Providence. The words of my father about accounting to God for gifts received were to haunt me for a long time because for me, at least, remorse was the offspring of guilt.

While undergoing treatment at the Hinsdale San, I took the first steps toward ceasing to dislike myself. Being comfortable with who I am—assigned to be just another writer who entertains instead of some sort of literary mahatma—will not be attained overnight, but now I am content with the ordinary role I was destined to play. For me this is progress. But I have not completely shaken the guilt. Not long ago I was reading, a glass of 7 Up in my hand, when someone knocked at the door. The first thing I did was to stash the glass behind the couch; in some misbegotten bit of reasoning, the 7 Up looked too much like vodka on the rocks. And it was just recently that, answering the telephone with a cold glass of soda pop in my hand, I held the glass at arm's length while talking because I did not want the caller to hear the tinkle of the ice cubes. This is distorted thinking, of course, and perhaps only time will dispel it.

During my last treatment I also achieved a certain serenity; it is not the serenity hoped for in a prayer adopted by most alcoholics—"the serenity to accept the things I cannot change, the courage to change the things I can, and the wisdom to know the difference"—but there is a beginning and that, too, is progress. And so is the acceptance that I was a sick, not an immoral, person. When I vowed so often that I would not drink again, I meant it at the time; I was not, as I feared, a liar. When a physical and psychological need is built up in the body, willpower can no more stop an alcoholic from catering to that need than it can stave off a stroke.

I have become resigned to loneliness being always a part of my life, but I think I've also learned to cope with it. I now understand that drinking will never banish loneliness; it only increases it.

I do not know if I will drink again. It would be nice to end this book by saying that I am cured. But that would be incorrect, because there is no cure. I still find it abhorrent to think that I cannot have a drink for the rest of my life. That is too dismal a prospect; it is better and easier to simply remind myself that I must not drink today. This, too, is progress, and progress is a good feeling.

There are many good feelings now, one of which is seeing a fellow sufferer regain his sobriety. I think of the alcoholic who related what made him throw his last bottle away. He used to spend whole afternoons in movie houses drinking in the dark, which meant frequent trips to the bathroom. At one point he stumbled back to his seat, unaware that he had neglected to zip up his pants. As he struggled along the aisle, the zipper somehow got caught in the hair of a lady sitting in front of him.

"I tugged and tugged," he said, "and the more we tugged the more hysterical she got. Finally I gave it one big jerk, and it happened—it was a wig and the damn thing came off, still attached to my zipper. Can you imagine how it feels to be escorted to the manager's office by an usher with a woman's wig hanging down there? They pretty near called the police."

I also think of another alcoholic, a friend, who tried making amends one night by taking his wife and children to a movie. "I don't know what was going through my head," he said, "but when the usher got us to the aisle, I stood aside to let the family in, then did the silliest thing I've ever done. I genuflected and made the sign of the cross! The crazy part is I was sober. I knew I wasn't in church, but I also knew it was time I got my reflexes straightened out."

And I think of the alcoholic who stopped drinking at the age of seventy-two. I asked him why he didn't leave things as they were for the years he had left. "Because," he snorted, "it was starting to interfere with my sex life." (Shakespeare touched on this in *Macbeth*, act 2: "It [drink] provokes the desire, but it takes away the performance.")

The three men stopped drinking for less than altruistic reasons, but I would never question their motives; I salute and envy their success.

Except for matrimony, I have never lived with a woman. I am doing so now. With ninety-seven women, to be exact.

After leaving the second halfway house where I had achieved ten months of total sobriety, I vowed I would never again live the communal life. I was proud of the soberness it had brought me, but I just did not like living with men. Many of them were slovenly in personal hygiene and table manners and, worse, they were bores. Some were ex-convicts who made it plain they used the halfway house route merely to speed up their parole or to impress their probation officer. During my stays at both halfway houses I found the three main subjects of conversation to be: (1) prison or police escapades, (2) panhandling and the price range of cheap wines, and (3) the care and maintenance of junk cars. At both places the most popular television program was something called "Hee Haw." Switching channels to a news program usually led to an argument.

This probably pegs me as an intellectual snob, but the only time the conversation flirted with culture was when one of the residents wandered into my room while I was at the typewriter. He spotted some of the books I had written and asked, "You make them things?"

"I write them," I said.

He pointed to the illustrations on the covers. "No, I mean the pictures. You make them pictures?"

"No. It's kind of hard to explain. I—"

"You sell them things too?"

"No, some other—"

"You don't often leave this place; you ain't selling 'em much?"

"No, I—"

He interrupted me again. "How can you sell books—you ain't even got a truck!" He stalked out, shaking his head.

In 1979, after what was hopefully my last attempt to do it my way—living alone—I decided to again venture into communal life. I had no options left, since I almost invariably returned to the barn when I was alone.

It had been hammered home to me that the alcoholic must be ready to do anything—including divorce or quitting a job—to maintain his sobriety. But I would not again live in a community of men.

That left just one alternative: women. It happens that I have always enjoyed the company of women, so the decision was appealing.

The ninety-seven women I live with—I call them my ninety-seven sisters—are the Sisters of St. Joseph, who operate Bethlehem Center, a multipurpose educational complex in La Grange Park, a suburb located fifteen miles west of Chicago. I had first come in contact with them years earlier, when I considered sending my children to their Nazareth Academy on the eighty-five-acre campus. I did not do this, because I felt that after taking eight grades in parochial schools the children should be exposed to the public system in high school in order to benefit from the viewpoint of "the others," as we used to call non-Catholics. Besides, I could not afford to finance eight children through another four years of private school.

The sisters and their pastoral environment had made an impression on me that had remained over the years. Bethlehem Center seemed to have some of the things I wanted. It was serene yet unsecluded; there was a venerableness about the buildings and grounds, and a devout zeal about its people. Their disinterest in the material things of life appealed to me, for I had become weary of the merry-go-round existence I had covered as a reporter and the hedonism I had hedgehopped in Hollywood, Chicago and New York for a quarter century. The place loomed as an ideal bower to write and think—yet never be alone—a haven for a man on the run, which I had become.

Something—was it a "higher power"?—told me to knock on the nuns' door. I did, and they took me in. It was a straightforward trade—my talents, whichever ways they could use them, for room and board. But for me there was a larger benefit—the companionship and inspiration of a 330-year-old religious order that had established itself in Illinois 82 years earlier.

Not to mention fringe benefits like a 150-foot-long outdoor swimming pool and tennis courts located in the shadow of a magnificent chapel through which I would have to walk at least six times a day to and from the dining room.

It had been three years since I had been to Mass. It was almost as long since I had experienced the sights and sounds of eight hundred laughing, yelling children—the students of Nazareth Academy. I was accustomed to the laughter of children—my own—and I missed it.

NINETEEN

I am surrounded by more than women. I am surrounded by talent.

As a youngster, before receiving Jesuit tutelage, I thought of nuns as religious people who did little but teach and pray, who perspired under layers of black clothing and whose exercise was limited to making the sign of the cross and rapping knuckles with a ruler hidden in their sleeve.

Most of the nuns I am with now have advanced academic degrees and function, both within and outside the school complex, in such fields as law, medicine, business, architecture, writing (books and magazines), public relations and the arts. There is a bank executive, an accountant, a hospital attorney, a women's prison advocate, a printer and a full-time chauffeur. Not to mention a bevy of counselors, cooks, gardeners, musicians, painters and sculptors.

Once I was informed that my apartment would be repainted. I expected regular tradesmen to do the job; instead, in trudged Sister Marlene Schemmel and Sister Pat Willems with paint cans and brushes. They not only looked like house painters, they painted like house painters. Sister Marlene was to be the vice president (formerly called assistant sister superior) of the order, and Sister Pat is a hospital chaplain who does cloisonné work and hooks tapestries on commission from business firms and institutions.

All of the statuary, oak carvings and plaster in the chapel and other buildings was created by the sisters on the premises. The stone mural behind the altar, consisting of twenty-two cast concrete panels, was created by Sister Richard Mehren, who teaches sculpture at Bethlehem's School of Art and carves tabernacles on commission. Sculpted in one-inch relief, it measures eight feet high and sixty-five feet wide. Its theme is the evolution of consciousness (the universe and all matter have been and are still undergoing constant change). The windows, comprising eleven thousand square feet of stained, hand-blown glass, were designed by Sister George Ellen Holmgren, who illustrates books on the side. A masterpiece of texture, color and surface movement, the stained-glass creation illustrates such themes as peace, sorrow, humility, hope and sacrifice. Sr. Mary Victoria Rokos, chapel organist, helped build the two-manual, stoplist tracker organ, a visual and aural masterwork. She also teaches voice and music, and is musical liturgy consultant to the Archdiocese of Chicago.

These are the women—who read professional and trade journals and follow world events closely—with whom I dine daily. I have never been at a loss for words, but I'm mortified at the number of times I've been stopped dead in conversation by the pros. The day after the Soviet Union invaded Afghanistan, I learned more at breakfast about the Persian Gulf community than I ever did at college. On the other hand, table talk with the nuns might easily commence with, "I stayed up late last night for that Joan Crawford movie and it wasn't worth it." (In my day they weren't even allowed to listen to the radio.)

One of the nuns I see often is Sister Mary Imelda (Victoria Kryger), who is in charge of the outdoor oratory in which the Our Lady of Lourdes grotto nestles. The grotto, a replica of the French original, was erected in 1940. It is made of tufa stone (dug up by the sisters on the property), measures thirty feet high, forty-three feet wide and twenty-two feet deep. Water cascades from the top of the cave to a basin at the feet of a figure of St. Bernadette. Amid an expanse of white oaks and black willows rising from honeysuckle shrubs, the grotto overlooks the calvary, the fourteen stone-sculpted Stations of the Cross depicting Christ's journey to the crucifixion.

Sister Mary Imelda is eighty-two, has all her teeth, and if she stands on her toes she can rise to a height of five feet. I first met her as she stood in a bed of marigolds and hyacinths, wondering what to do about the impudence of her "little friends." The grotto is on the edge of a forest preserve and her "friends" include white-tail deer forever munching on the jonquils, a family of woodchucks that had moved into the grotto, and a robin nesting at the Third Station of the Cross ("Jesus Falls for the First Time").

"I feel guilty," she said. "I was going to tend to the daffodils—see how they're drooping?—and I've spent most of my time talking to the foxes."

She was perspiring, and well she should, because she is one of only two nuns at Bethlehem Center who wear the original habit: black robe, headdress complete with cornet and veil, and a crucifix dangling below the guimpe (bib). This is in contrast to the others, who wear a modified habit —headdress with skirt, pantsuits or conventional dresses— or even blue jeans and open-toed sandals on weekends.

"This is the way I received the habit," she explained, "and this is the way I want to stay. I don't have to look for my identity; I know I am the bride of Christ. Can you imagine me in a pantsuit?"

"But isn't that long black robe a little hot in the summer?" I asked.

"So what?" she shot back. "It's drip-dry and just takes fifteen minutes to wash. Anyway, the ten pleats on the habit represent the Ten Commandments, and don't you think the world needs to be reminded of that?"

Sometimes Sister Mary Imelda does remind the world. When Pope John Paul II visited Chicago, she wangled reserved tickets for the Mass at Grant Park, hitched a ride to Chicago, found a policeman who put her on a bus to the park, charmed another officer into a squad car ride to the train station after the Mass, and when she got off at La Grange Park a man and woman, total strangers, offered her a lift home. "Do you think I could have done that in blue jeans?" she smiled. "I stormed heaven to see this wonderful pope from my homeland, and I got all that attention because of the habit. People were stopping me on the street and saying, 'We want to shake the hand of a real sister.'"

She stood up after patting a wisp of violets and pointed to a Black girl seated beneath a red cedar. "She's in fourth grade," she said, "and she likes to help me around the grotto, but she keeps calling it the ghetto!"

From my unique vantage point I have been able to observe some reaction to the shifts in the Catholic Church, the changes in the liturgy and the new liberality in mode and mores. There is a thin line of disparity, a nuance of posture, and the line is marked off by age. Generally, the nuns over sixty prefer "the way it used to be" and view with some disquiet the modernized way of life of those in their twenties and thirties. When I was a youngster, a nun never ventured out alone; today she drives hither and yon and need not ask permission to go cycling or visit the hairdresser. When I was young the nuns told us that

movies often brought the risk of sin; I never thought I'd
see the day when nuns would ask if I'd go to the movies
with them.

Certainly, there is no "taking sides" in this matter between the young and old schools of religious life. The older
generation tolerates the fact that younger sisters pluck
their eyebrows, wear summer shorts (but not in the classroom) and don't have to attend daily Mass as was once the
norm. They recognize that today's nun is not the same as
that of yesteryear, who made the decision to enter religious
life while still in high school.

But they are so human. When I started school, a nun
who would dare to smoke was unheard of, so I was taken
aback when a young nun told me she would give up smoking during Lent. After three weeks she borrowed a cigarette
from me and sighed, "I just can't make it." In a way, that
incident gave me some solace: If a nun had that problem
with cigarette addiction, my alcoholic relapses should not
make me hate myself as much as I did. (Incidentally, the
alcoholic nuns described in Chapter Eleven are not con-
nected with the group with which I am now living.)

I suppose my first inkling that nuns were indeed very
human occurred one morning shortly after I came to Bethlehem Center. I was walking through the chapel, where
they were attending six o'clock Mass, en route to the dining room and the day's first coffee. As usual, I had the
morning paper under my arm and I heard a "psst." A nun
was waving me over. I walked to the pew and leaned over
to hear her whisper, "What did the Cubs do last night?"
When I told her the score—surely the only man ever to report a sports event while genuflecting—I noticed she was
following Mass with a Latin missal instead of using the
English-language liturgy.

I soon discovered that the Chicago Cubs have an inordinate number of fans among the sisters of St. Joseph. A typical rooter is Sister Cyril Caron, who has been following the Cub members' destinies for thirty-two years. Sister Caron, who once headed the laundry brigade, owns a baseball autographed by the team and never misses a game on television. "When the Cubs are playing," she said, "I close my door. That's the sign that the sisters are not to bother me when the game is on." I could not bring myself to ask if she and her fellow sisters ever prayed for their team; after all, the Cubs have not won a pennant since 1945.

One day at lunch the talk drifted to a Cub loss the night before, when the Los Angeles Dodgers nudged Chicago out of first place. The Cubs had been beaten by Dodger pitcher Bob Welch, who had gone the full nine innings. Coincidentally, the morning papers had carried a long story about alcoholic baseball players, including Welch and Kansas City Royals catcher Darrell Porter, who had "gone public" with their problem and were undergoing treatment. I casually mentioned the story to the sisters. "Well," one of them chirped, "Welch certainly wasn't drinking last night; he almost shut us out."

Welch had said he did not think he was an alcoholic, "but I learned about myself. It was painful, but I'm more proud of this than anything I've ever done. What others might think is their problem, not mine."

Porter, who was the American League's all-star catcher in 1979, told reporters at a press conference, "My whole life was being affected. Some time ago I decided I was tired of the shape I was in and I wasn't going to have it anymore."

Don Newcombe, former Dodger pitcher and admitted alcoholic, who heads the Dodger alcoholic rehabilitation program, was instrumental in getting Welch into treatment. He speculates that up to 15 percent of the professional ball players are alcoholics: "Baseball players must realize that we are living in an alcohol and drug culture. It's easily available to them. They can get all the beer they want right there in the clubhouse. Professional sports have not stressed the importance and seriousness of this problem."

Another baseball great who is helping players with their problem is former Yankee pitcher Ryne Duren. The hard-throwing right-hander tours the country making speeches for the National Council on Alcoholism. "I started drinking at fourteen," he recalled. "I had a drinking problem through all my teens and through the minor leagues and on through the big leagues. It was kind of an insidious thing that just gained on me all the time."

Dr. Gerald Rozansky, a Los Angeles psychiatrist who has treated professional athletes, cited the characteristic of denial as being acute among alcoholics in the public eye. "Athletes are nothing special. They have pressure and frequent travel, but everyone is pressured by something. Yet I would say that athletes have a particular denial problem. If they're top-notch, as long as they can score points, nobody gets too excited about the rest of their lives. This adds to the denial."

Denial worked differently for Dennis Lick, twenty-six-year-old offensive tackle with the Chicago Bears, who, in May 1980, hospitalized himself for alcoholism and made it public. Lick said he knew he had a problem but, "People never wanted to say anything. They would say, 'Just take it easy; you can drink once in a while.' Even today they don't think I have a problem. A big thing was expectation. Being a big guy and a professional football player, you were expected to be a drinker, a wild guy. When you're big and strong you think you can do things all by yourself."

The pressures mentioned by athletes tie in with a thought on that aspect expressed by Dr. Morris Chafetz:

"The demands of the work and the nature of the exposure to alcohol are frequently at fault. Studies show that the set and circumstances under which we drink may have more to do with developing problems than individual psychological needs alone. Certain professions are highly tension-producing, with drinking very much part of the scene. Such professions are theater, writing, television, magazine and newspaper work—jobs with tight deadlines, public exposure and the pressure to excel. We do not know whether the profession causes the individual's alcohol problem, or whether he or she chooses the profession that makes it easy to develop alcoholism."

So, in a way, the wheel of my life has come full circle. I went from my mother's knee to the nuns when I was five years old, and I am back with them again. They are a sort of refuge, and I feel I have come home again.

After turning away from God—I never turned my back—because of anger, false pride and doubt, I've come to recognize my need for a resumption of spirituality. Here I am practically a part of it. Indeed, I can't escape the aura of sanctity, whether it's in the sisters' joyous alleluias wafting from the chapel, their swinging band coaxing trombone, bass, piano, guitar, banjo and drums into ragtime (they call themselves the Pink Garter and even play benefits for Protestant churches), or playing bingo with the older ones (so far I've won two pairs of earrings, a box of hair curlers and a hand-knitted shawl).

Overall, it has become easier to pray. Before I learned that alcoholism was a disease, I found it difficult to pray for help. What was the use? Getting drunk was immoral and I was embarrassed to talk to God about it. Besides, it would be ludicrous. The world usually seemed set to go up

in flames; in some lands starving people ate rats and home-
less children slept in open fields. They deserved God's attention more than I did, so how could he bother himself
with that drunk out there, too weak or stupid to do what he
had to do, which was simply to stop?

I was too ashamed to go directly to God, so with the alcoholic's typical cunning I substituted my parents as stand-
ins: If there was a heaven, my mother and father had to be
there, and certainly they had clout. So I took the rounda-
bout route and prayed to them instead to be my surrogates
and use their influence.

*I would say, "Dad, what's happened? This isn't the way
it was supposed to turn out. Why can't things be the way
they were? You're there. I need help. Would you put in a
word for me?"*

Early one morning I walked to the grotto just as the sun
was coming up. It made me feel warm to watch it because,
as a practicing alcoholic, I had forgotten what a sunrise
looked like. A pair of ducks in vivid nuptial plumage wad-
dled by, and overhead a restless oriole darted to its hanging
nest. I found myself at the Third Station of the Cross
depicting Jesus felled by the weight of his burden. Inexpli-
cably I wandered to the seventh, where he stumbled for
the second time, and then to the ninth, where he slumped
for the third time. I don't know where it came from, but
suddenly it struck me that there was a message coming to
me from the stone sculptures: Man will fall—once, three
times, a hundred times—but the important thing is that he
get up and keep going. That message has led me to judge
myself now not by my failures but by my efforts. "We are
healed of a suffering," Marcel Proust wrote, "only by ex-
periencing it to the full."

For a long time I had looked upon prayer as a socially ac-
ceptable harbor in which to take refuge from tempests.

But, watching the sisters of St. Joseph doing service in the church to the world outside, I now know that real prayer is in action. And action, for the alcoholic, is not *drinking*. That, one day at a time, is his prayer.

Today I possess sobriety—by this I mean that I am not drinking today—and I attribute it to a return to spirituality, inspiration from the "winners" in Alcoholics Anonymous, my rapport with Dr. Anderson, striving to know and understand and like myself, but, more important, being thoroughly honest with myself.

It is something of a paradox that learning to like myself has been difficult despite my alcoholic ego. But the Hinsdale San's Dr. Anderson made it easier with a strange prescription: "I want you to take your awards and plaques," he said, "and hang them up on your wall."

"Whatever for?" I asked.

"It'll be good for you to look at them when you go to bed at night and first thing in the morning. They'll remind you of what you were—and what you can be again."

I hung up two or three, and with them I hung a maxim which I'd had for years. I didn't know who authored it, but I had become very fond of it:

YESTERDAY . . . TODAY . . . TOMORROW

"There are two days in every week about which we should not worry, two days which should be kept free from fear and apprehension.

"One of these days is YESTERDAY, with its mistakes and cares, its faults and blunders, its aches and pains. YESTERDAY has passed forever beyond our control.

"All the money in the world cannot bring back YESTERDAY. We cannot undo a single act we performed; we cannot erase a single word we said . . . YESTERDAY is gone.

"The other day we should not worry about is TOMORROW, with its possible adversaries, its burdens, its large promise and poor performance. TOMORROW is also beyond our immediate control.

"TOMORROW's sun will rise, either in splendor or behind a mask of clouds, but it will rise. Until it does, we have no stake in TOMORROW, for it is as yet unborn.

"This leaves only one day—TODAY. Any man can fight the battle of just one day. It is only when you and I add the burdens of those two awful eternities—YESTERDAY and TOMORROW —that we break down. It is not the experience of TODAY that drives men mad . . . It is the remorse or bitterness for something which happened YESTERDAY and the dread of what TO-MORROW will bring.

"Let us therefore live but one day at a time!"

The awards have come down from the wall, but the maxim is still there.